MS. MAYOR:
How Republicans and my Ex-husband Tried to Ruin My Life

Marni Sawicki
Peter Golenbock

While this book is intended to provide accurate and up-to-date information, because the potential for civil or criminal appeals, it's impossible to ensure all the information provided is accurate at the time of publication.

All rights reserved. No part of this book may be used or reproduced in any form whatsoever without written permission except in the case of brief quotations in critical articles or reviews.

Printed in the United States of America.

For more information, or to book an event, contact:
marni@marnisawicki.com
https://www.MsMayorTheBook.com

Written by Marni Sawicki and Peter Golenbock
Editing by Peter Golenbock
Cover design by Adedolapo Ogungbire
Cover photo by Erika Larsen for *Politico Magazine*
Beta Reading/Proofreading by Hannah Skaggs

ISBN – Paperback: 979-8-88796-005-0
ISBN – Hardcover: 979-8-88796-006-7
ISBN – Electronic : 979-8-88796-009-8

First Edition: November 2022

Copyright © 2022 by Marni Sawicki and Peter Golenbock.

MS. MAYOR

To my children, Madisson and Brendon.
You are the light that keeps me going.

MARNI SAWICKI & PETER GOLENBOCK

Contents

CHAPTER 1 The General Election 1

CHAPTER 2 The Decision to Run 14

CHAPTER 3 The Primary Election 34

CHAPTER 4 Dating While in Office 50

CHAPTER 5 Opponents Demand Recounts 72

CHAPTER 6 The Restraining Order 94

CHAPTER 7 Getting Things Done 112

CHAPTER 8 The School Principal Was a Crook 136

CHAPTER 9 Getting Married 151

CHAPTER 10 If All Else Fails, Throw Dirt 163

CHAPTER 11 An Internal Investigation 182

CHAPTER 12 The Critics Chime In 188

CHAPTER 13 Punches to the Face 203

CHAPTER 14 Irma 221

CHAPTER 15 The FDLE Investigation 239

CHAPTER 16 Breaking Free 249

About the Authors 270

MARNI SAWICKI & PETER GOLENBOCK

Acknowledgments

Without my children, Madisson and Brendon, this book would never have been written. Their love and support sustained me during some of the darkest days of my life.

To Susie Zimmer and Kelvin Thompkins: You've been there for me the entire time with your unwavering support, and I am so very grateful for our friendship. You both picked me up, dusted me off, and gave me strength when I needed it most.

To my parents, who taught me about resilience and getting back up when you fall: Your love and generosity made it possible for me to heal.

To Greg Bennett: You've spent many late nights listening to me talk about this book and loved me through the pain of writing it. Thank you.

To my beautiful mentor, Michel Doherty: Thank you for always having faith in me and teaching me how important it is to lift women up. I know you are watching over me and guiding me from above.

To my beautiful sorority sisters of Sigma Sigma Sigma: Thank you for your love and concern. So many friendships have stood the test of time.

Finally, to Peter Golenbock: Thank you for helping me make this book a reality.

CHAPTER 1

THE GENERAL ELECTION

Success is not final; failure is not fatal: it is the courage to continue that counts. —Winston S. Churchill

As I stood there waiting for the election results to come in, I looked around the bar, taking in the electricity of it all. The date was November 5, 2013, the day of the general election, and I was running to become the first woman mayor of Cape Coral—at the time, the tenth-largest city in Florida.

Win or lose, I was proud because our campaign had been a positive one. My platform consisted of three core messages: increase the transparency and accountability of city government, strengthen our local economy, and improve our community's quality of life.

When I moved to Cape Coral in 2011, I was forty-one years old, and the average age of the population there was forty-three, but because the city was made up of only 8 percent commercial business, finding friends within my age range or places to meet them was difficult. With a politically active mother, I was taught at a very young age that if you don't like something, change it. It's that simple.

I wanted more for my city. Because it had no downtown, we needed a destination place—a gathering place for shopping, eating, playing, and living.

My opponent, incumbent mayor John Sullivan, who was seventy years old, fought to keep the city small. He wanted everything there to stay the same (or even go back a few years).

Sullivan was part of a group called the Cape Coral Minutemen, Republicans who prided themselves on fighting against policies leading to what they viewed as out-of-control government spending.

What this group was really trying to do was keep the city from growing. Sullivan and a core group of powerful city leaders wanted total and absolute control over local policymaking. Even though the city was one of the largest in Florida, this group fought to keep out new residents. They did it by turning down county money to improve bridges, fighting over county toll road money to pave the roads, and never understanding how to get their fair share of county money.

Those who ran Cape Coral for years wanted it to remain a small bedroom community with the lights out at dusk. The Cape Coral Minutemen did their best to accomplish just that, hoping to deter people from moving to the city. In their refusal to upgrade Veterans Highway with flyovers, they lost over $40 million in state and county funding. This one decision will haunt the city for decades.

The powers that be were happy to keep the city isolated. They refused to take leadership positions in organizations like the Florida League of Cities. For them, the isolation of Cape Coral was a sign of its independence. From what I could see, their refusal to allow the city to grow was small-minded and counterproductive. I was determined to run against these obstructionists and do what I could to transform Cape Coral into the great, modern city it deserves to be.

Sullivan's entire campaign platform was based on his belief that the city needed to continue to tighten its belt and rein in spending.

For the first two years he was in office, Sullivan and his crew of four other council members decimated the city budget, leaving our roads and bridges in desperate need of repair. City employees had not received raises in seven years, and police and fire equipment broke down daily. The police department had volunteers going out each morning to jump-start police vehicles so they would be ready for the morning shifts.

At the Chamber of Commerce debate, Sullivan and I were given the opportunity to ask each other a question.

"There isn't anything I can learn from her," said Sullivan.

"How have you contributed to the commercial growth of the city?" I asked him.

He stammered on about issues city staff had pushed for but never gave a clear example of how he had effected any changes.

As soon as he finished, I said to him, "Mayor, I didn't ask what others have done to grow our commercial base; I asked what *you* have personally done to facilitate growth."

Audience members began laughing. Sullivan was furious. One of his supporters wrote to Joe Mazurkiewicz, the chairman of the Chamber of Commerce, insisting that I openly apologize for my "out-of-control supporters."

Mazurkiewicz, the longest-seated mayor in the city's history, wrote back saying no apology was warranted.

From the start, Sullivan insisted my candidacy did not worry him. He made that clear when he spoke in public, was quoted in the news, or spoke to me directly. We had a debate on the Drew Steel morning radio show. I sat across from him, and during a commercial break, he said, "After I beat you, I will date you."

He did not beat me, nor did he ever get the chance to date me. I made sure of that.

I was used to that kind of misogyny. As a rare woman working at a leading specialty property and casualty insurance company, I was constantly having to find ways to fit in with the boys' club. I even started golfing so I could be present for some of their most important client meetings.

During one of my reviews, my boss spoke to me about my work attire.

"You need to dress more conservatively," he said.

It was casual Friday during the wintertime. I asked if what I was wearing was appropriate.

"With what I have on," I said, "only my head and hands are showing."

"I have a tough time looking you in the eyes," he said, "because of your blouse. Something needs to change."

"I thought that's where you are supposed to look at me . . . in my eyes," I said.

"You need to dress more like Janice in accounting," he said.

Janice always wore a gray pantsuit.

I would be fired for not fitting in, so I hired a civil rights attorney to represent me for wrongful termination. My company offered me two weeks' severance in return for signing a nondisclosure document.

I declined. My attorney sent over a few pages of my journal as evidence showing instances of sexual harassment. We settled out of court.

On election night, my staff and I hosted our watch party at a bar called the Dixie Roadhouse. I had become close with the owner, Lynn Pippenger, and we were hoping the evening would be a night of celebration. I had spent most of the day speeding between precincts, talking to as many people as I could. I knew the vote would be close because in the primary election, only 8 percent of registered voters had turned out.

The evening was already extra special as my parents had flown in from my hometown the night before to be there for the election. I could see the pride in their eyes as people came up to talk to them throughout the evening. Two other candidates for District 6 and District 4, incumbent councilman Kevin McGrail and candidate Richard Leon, also held their watch parties there as well.

Both sought to wrest control of the city from the incumbent mayor and his cronies.

Cape Coral has had a long history of contentious elections. The city was incorporated in 1970, and I love the fact that I was born that same year.

We made it through the primary on a campaign budget of just $12,000. Overall, we raised $33,000, a far cry from the $85,000 I was told we needed to even be a threat.

Because I was a Democrat, many Cape Coral residents told me they couldn't donate to my campaign for fear that they would be ostracized for being named on my campaign report.

Brian Rist, the owner of Storm Smart, a company that manufactures hurricane shutters and one of the largest employers in the county, was an important supporter. He was a Republican, and even though it was a nonpartisan race, having his name on my finance reports helped lower the apprehension among his fellow Republicans who had an issue with voting for a Democrat.

After I won the primary election, the heat turned up almost immediately. Cape Coral residents were excited because we had run such a positive campaign. There was no way we were going to let anyone divert us from my message: if I became mayor, my goal was to breathe new life into Cape Coral.

While the election was nonpartisan, a large contingency of my opponents preferred to make it partisan. The city was predominantly Republican, and in 2016 Cape Coral became Trump Republican.

Mayor John Sullivan had the full force of the Lee County Republican Party behind him. Two Republican political action committees helped send out disinformation about my campaign. The first mailer had a terrible photo of me on the front and spelled my name wrong. The caption read, "Marni Sawiki may have trouble telling voters what she stands for. But we know what Cape Coral would look like if she were mayor: More taxes. More bureaucracy. More fees. More government regulations."

The second of the three mailers was set up like a comic strip with three photos of Sullivan and me from the Chamber of Commerce debate on the front. There was a wide red line on the left, where Sullivan was sitting, saying "Conservatives." On the right of the mailer was a wide blue line with "Liberals"

written in larger lettering near where I was sitting. The heading said, "Cape Coral Mayoral Race."

The comic showed captions coming from our mouths. In the first picture, Sullivan was saying, "Marni, Some people say you have taken all sides on this issue . . ." In the next photo, a caption coming from me said, "Precisely!" The third picture showed another bubble from me saying, "I now have the issue surrounded!"

My team was composed of people from every party, and I worked hard to get the cross-over votes. I had also received the endorsements of every organization in town, from the *News-Press* newspaper to the Cape Coral Construction Industry Association (CCCIA), the Cape Coral Real Estate Board, and the Chamber of Commerce.

Cape Coral residents were ready for a new kind of politics—forward-looking liberal politics—and I was ready to give it to them.

On the evening of the general election, representatives from all seven unions were present at the Dixie Roadhouse to watch the results come in. Had Sullivan been a more moderate mayor, I don't think I would have won. The Republicans who supported me quietly were doing so not because they wanted me, but because they no longer wanted Sullivan. We had just come out of a recession, and Cape Coral was number one in the country for foreclosed homes—ground zero. Residents were eager to turn the page, and having Sullivan in office, they felt, would hinder the city's progress.

As the watch party got started at Dixie Roadhouse, country music echoed throughout the bar as people line-danced, ate, and reminisced about the campaign. The website of the supervisor of elections, which gave the results, was projected on a large screen.

The cutoff for voting was 7:00 p.m., and the time was drawing near. In past elections, results had come in extremely fast. The media predicted a turnout of 17 percent of all registered voters. Only 8 percent had voted in the primary election—7,743 out of 101,951 registered voters in the city.

On this final day of voting in the general election, the mood was electric. Even though I was surrounded by my supportive campaign team, I felt sick to my stomach. All our hard work had brought us to this day.

The suspense was almost too much to bear. When the results started coming in, the numbers showed that Councilmember Kevin McGrail, one of the good guys who wanted to see change in Cape Coral, had lost his reelection bid.

He was up against Rick Williams, who was close to the incumbent mayor and past council members. Williams represented the old guard, and I was sad that Kevin had lost to him.

On the other hand, I was pleased to see that Richard Leon defeated the incumbent, Chris Chulakes-Leetz, in his council race. Leon, a young and up-and-coming candidate, had won a close primary election. It was encouraging that he beat Chulakes-Leetz with 58 percent of the vote.

My team huddled around me, waiting anxiously for the results of the mayoral race. Seven o'clock seemed an eternity away.

As the precincts refreshed their numbers, the race was still too close to call. It was even closer than we could have imagined. As the results came in, my team stood in a circle around me, holding hands.

The TV cameras started coming in the door of the bar, and I could feel the excitement growing. As everyone stood staring at the screen, the results from the supervisor of elections website popped up on the screen . . .

Final. "All Precincts Reporting," it said. As if in slow motion, the crowd of a few hundred people erupted into a roar.

I had won . . . by 121 votes. We were all in shock.

Celebrating with supporters after winning the General Election.

I received 50.36 percent of the vote. To trigger an automatic recount, the vote needed to be within a 0.05 percent margin. Since I received 0.72 percent more than Sullivan, there would be no recount.

The eruption sounded more like a reaction to a Super Bowl victory than an election watch party. Supporters were yelling, jumping up and down, crying, and hugging each other. Katy Perry's song "Roar" blared on the sound system.

Taking the microphone, I thanked my supporters.

"Today begins a new era in politics for Cape Coral," I said. "Gone are the days of the city going to sleep at 8:00 p.m. Thanks to all your hard work, we will put Cape Coral on the map! Tomorrow, we start anew!"

My speech was short, but I made sure to mention every one of the key members of my campaign. I surely would have lost without their support and their boots on the ground.

My beloved city had spoken. The residents were ready for something new and for *someone* new—and that person was me. I was unfiltered, unapologetic, and unafraid to speak my mind.

I left the bar and went outside to meet with reporters. I brought a half dozen of my key team members to stand with me. We held hands as the reporter asked his questions.

Watching the pride on everyone's faces brought the night to a wonderful end. Ex-mayor John Sullivan, arrogant and entitled, never called to congratulate me.

The rest of the evening was a whirlwind. Between shaking hands, taking photos, and doing TV interviews, I did not have time to let the win sink in.

Before the night ended, word had already gotten around that Sullivan was demanding a recount. The Republicans, who cared about nothing but winning, dedicated themselves to making the next four years of my life as miserable as they could.

CHAPTER 2

THE DECISION TO RUN

It takes courage to grow up and become who you really are. —E.E. Cummings

I never grew up thinking about running for elected office—at any level. Even with my mother so active in politics, the thought never crossed my mind. While running for office was not top of mind, volunteering and being active in charities has always been a passion. To explain how I came to run for mayor, I need to first give you some background on who I was growing up.

I was born February 16, 1970, in Battle Creek, Michigan. My father worked at the Kellogg Company as a millwright for thirty-seven years. My mother worked in social services, was a civilian secretary for the Michigan Air National Guard, and, after being elected to recording secretary, worked for almost two decades for the United Auto Workers union at the state level.

We were a union household.

I was raised to never underestimate what a small group of people can accomplish. There is power in standing united. I realized this the very first time my father went on strike. Kellogg's employees started picketing in the early 1970s and the strike lasted almost a month. Even though I was very young, that moment has been forever engraved in my mind. The stress was all over my parents' face. No one knew how long the strike would last, and the company was hiring people (scabs) to take the place of those picketing. The men and women who stood their ground did not know if they would have a job to go back to; however, they persevered. At home, we ate Spam, which is canned meat that is sliced and fried, to save money. My mother reheated day-old boxed macaroni and cheese by adding a little milk to make the food stretch as long as possible. Eventually, the company and union came to an agreement. Even when I grew up and started working in corporate America, I never forgot the lesson of safety in numbers.

My mother also won a seat on the Pennfield School Board, where she served for ten years. I would help her by going door-to-door to pass out campaign literature. She was always active in our local and state election campaigns. My freshman year of high school, I ran for my first elected seat and won secretary of my class. It's amazing to think about those years I campaigned. I was born Marni Dilsaver, and I made homemade pins in the shape of a dill pickle that said, "Vote for Dilsaver." I held that position all four years of high school.

We lived a middle-class life with all the expected difficulties of family life. Having grown up during the time of the Great Depression, my grandparents were strict. Both of my grandfathers were veterans, one in the army and the other in the navy. My paternal grandfather was a Golden Glove boxer in the navy. He did not let having four granddaughters stand in the way of teaching us to box. I was taught to be grateful for the men and women who serve(d) our country.

I understood at an early age that we were fortunate to have our freedom but that the freedom we enjoyed came at a high cost. My grandmother lost her brother, who was manning the torpedoes on the USS *Houston* during the bombing of Pearl Harbor. Each year we would visit his grave that showed he was missing in action (MIA) along with other family members who served.

My grandmother would tell us stories of her life growing up. She lived to be one hundred years old. Growing up in Mississippi near the Tishomingo Indian reservation, she had plenty of fascinating stories of how the Indians taught her people to survive and, in turn, they shared their goods and newest inventions with them. After she married my grandfather, they flew his Cessna airplane from Michigan to Mississippi. My grandfather took the chief up on his first-ever flight. She could tell the story in such a way, I felt like I had been there.

Growing up, we attended the North Avenue Church of God in Pennfield. My mother, my sister, and I went there every Sunday morning, Sunday evening, and Wednesday for youth group. I was later married in that church, and my daughter was christened there. Church was especially important to my mother, and I attended faithfully until I went off to college. I have always believed in a higher power, but a very bad childhood experience at church made me realize I could be close to God without needing to worship every Sunday.

When I was sixteen, my girlfriend tried to commit suicide at school. We were inseparable at church and at school since I had moved to the school in third grade. Scared, I called 911 and she was taken to the hospital and eventually moved into a psychiatric hospital for few months to be observed. I could only see her when her parents brought her to church on Sundays while she was in the hospital. One Sunday, in front of the entire church, her parents singled me out and started screaming at me for calling 911. Her mother was a teacher and I had embarrassed her by calling while at school. I was humiliated, and while I do understand now it was their grief speaking, I did not look forward to attending after that. Over the years, I have come to terms with my feelings surrounding this incident.

The athletic gene skipped over me, and I instead chose reading, art, theater, and playing the flute as my hobbies. I loved my art classes. My art teacher, Mr. Tom Tenney, was one of my favorite teachers. I was always proud when one of my art pieces earned a prize at a local art fair. A close second was my government teacher, Mr. John Baxter. He loved teaching civics class. I enjoyed learning about how the United States came to be. He taught us that history is doomed to repeat if we do not learn from past mistakes. I learned to look deeper into why a policy or law was put in place and came to understand that sometimes the original law required change as times change.

I started playing the flute when I was in middle school and practiced for hours each day. Music has always been my way of escaping reality. As stress increased at home, I found myself playing more and more. Playing that much paid off as I sat as first chair for four years of high school. I loved playing; however, once I graduated, I never picked up a flute again.

I was raped when I was fifteen. I never told anyone but my best friend. I was unable to talk about this for decades.

My sophomore year, I applied for a scholarship from the Kellogg company to go overseas as an exchange student. I was picked to go to Denmark for an eight-week summer program with a group called Youth for Understanding.

Back then, we did not have cell phones, mail took weeks to deliver, and international landline phone calls cost several dollars a minute, so once I left, I was alone until the day I returned. If I was not already independent when I left, I certainly returned that way.

For my flight home, we boarded a double-decker Jumbo DC-10 bound for JFK International Airport. There were about fifty exchange students on board. I had a window seat just above the wing of the airplane.

I sat next to a girlfriend, and we were chatting as the plane took off. I glanced out the window and asked her, "Are there supposed to be flames coming out of the engine?"

Just then the captain came over the loudspeaker.

"Ladies and gentlemen, please remain calm. We have a small emergency. We will be returning to the airport, but first, we must dump forty metric tons of fuel."

The entire flight got eerily quiet. I grabbed the hand of the girl next to me. There was a lot of turbulence, but the cabin and crew remained calm. It was happening so fast, no one really knew what to say.

As we came in for the landing, we could see the flashing lights of the emergency personnel. We landed safely. It was not until we started to get off the plane that we fully understood the gravity of the situation. We could have died.

I ended up on the front page of the Copenhagen newspaper along with the girl I had sat next to. The headline read, "Terror in the Sky!"

We were not allowed to call our parents, and I had no idea whether they even knew there had been an issue. All fifty exchange students had to sleep in the airport that evening.

When I was reunited with my parents at the Detroit Metro Airport, the only thing my father said to me was, "What the hell is in your nose?" That summer had changed me. I had grown up overnight, it seemed. I had learned to rely on myself to get through the tough times. The internet was not in widespread use until my sophomore year of college. We are certainly more connected now with our computers, cell phones, and smart watches.

I kept the earring in my nose for only a couple of weeks. The fad did not make it to the United States for a few decades.

I went from high school to Central Michigan University in Mount Pleasant, Michigan. I was lucky enough to be hired by the Kellogg Company, working in the factory during the summers. Working in the summer allowed me to save enough money to pay for the upcoming school year along with my rent and utilities. While there, I became a union employee and was trained as a line assistant where they packaged the cereal. I sometimes ran into my father if I worked the third shift. He never really said much other than to give me a nod. That summer job gave me the strength to keep going to college—even when I didn't like going. The alternative was to work in the factory, and I knew I wanted more for myself.

College was a blur. My very first semester, I rushed a sorority called Sigma Sigma Sigma and was offered a bid. There I met friends who would last me a lifetime. While I had many acquaintances in high school, here is where I learned what real friendship is. I met my best friend Mary during bid day. We lived together every year until she graduated. We were both in each other's weddings, and even as life happened, we did not lose touch.

I was incredibly honored when my sorority asked me to be their keynote speaker for our seventy-fifth anniversary celebration in 2017. I gave a speech about the importance of living an authentic life and how, by doing that, we give others permission to live theirs. As women, we were taught by our families to be seen but not heard. I can hear all the limiting beliefs in my head still to this day: be humble, don't gloat, women are too emotional, you need a man in order to live a good life, and the list goes on. As the years went by, I slowly learned how to maneuver through this world as a woman. With each new position, I grew more and more confident in my abilities.

Studying never came easy for me (until I started my MBA). My first year of college was mostly partying, so much so that I ended up being placed on academic probation and returning home to Battle Creek for a semester to study at Kellogg Community College.

"Once you leave school, you never go back," everyone told me.

But I was hell-bent on proving them wrong. After one semester, I returned to Central Michigan University with a renewed sense of purpose. Many times in my life, I have had the wind knocked out of me, but I have never let that hold me down.

I always get back up.

I took a job as a cocktail server at the Holiday Inn in Midland while finishing school. There I fell in love with Adam Sawicki, a bartender and one of the kindest men I have ever met.

I graduated from college in 1993 and received a job offer from WBCK radio station in Battle Creek, Michigan.

In a short time, Adam and I both moved to Battle Creek, my hometown. He formally proposed to me at a place called the Waterfront Restaurant.

While selling airtime, I had a client who was a State Farm agent. We immediately hit it off. After I had collaborated with her for about a month as her marketing representative, she offered me a job that paid a few thousand more a year than I was currently making. I jumped at the opportunity.

I enjoyed working in the agency, but I wanted to do more than just take auto applications. The home office was where I really wanted to be. Not more than a year later, I interviewed with State Farm Insurance Companies in Marshall, Michigan, as an auto underwriter.

They hadn't hired anyone in over a year and a half. The interview consisted of three panel interviews with six supervisors and managers. During the interview, one of the managers asked me about my GPA.

"I see you only have a 2.9 GPA," he said.

"Yes," I said.

"Do you think that's good enough to be hired at State Farm?"

"Well," I said, "I took eighteen credit hours a semester, was active with my social sorority, and worked forty hours a week to support myself, all so I could be that well-rounded student everyone wants. So, yes, I think it is good enough."

He just nodded and wrote something down. I left the interview positive I had blown it. But two days later, I received a call from Human Resources.

The woman who called chuckled when she told me I had gotten the job as an underwriter. When I asked what was so funny, she replied, "I don't know. You just seem like you would fit better in claims."

I took that to mean I had a big personality. Only two people were hired from this group of about thirty: Debra Moon and me. The two of us became incredible friends. My salary was $23,260. I couldn't have been happier. I started work one week after being married.

Adam and I married on November 5, 1995. I would have preferred a small wedding on a beach somewhere, but Adam wanted a big wedding. He comes from an exceptionally large family. His mother had ten brothers and sisters. It was your typical very tight-knit Polish family. They were so close that every Christmas they would rent banquet rooms at the Holiday Inn and all his aunts, uncles, cousins, etc. would stay for the weekend, swimming and barbecuing. Coming from a small family, I was overwhelmed the whole weekend, but looking back, I am grateful that I got to experience it.

Starting my new job at State Farm was exciting. Having a solid job allowed Adam and me to purchase a small starter home in Battle Creek. The home was only nine hundred square feet, but it was perfect for the two of us.

I was pregnant a year later, and Madisson was born June 8, 1997. She was the most beautiful baby I had ever seen. Of course, every parent says that, but since she was two weeks late, she came out with a full head of blonde hair and the most beautiful blue eyes. Every nurse who came into the room seemed shocked at just how striking she was. The bond that was created that day between her and me has never been broken. To this day, she is not just my daughter but my best friend. Family is important to me.

In January 1997, a position opened up with State Farm in Atlanta, Georgia. They were closing two offices and combining their Georgia, South Carolina, Alabama, and Mississippi offices. The headquarters would be based in Atlanta.

Debra and I both applied for the position. There were only twenty-five positions available, and people throughout the United States were applying. To our shock and surprise, both of us were selected. We planned to move in July. My parents were heartbroken that we would be taking their only granddaughter to another state, but I was so excited for the opportunity. To top it off, no more snow!

Adam and I built a new home in Dacula, Georgia. It was so much bigger than our home in Michigan. The house was built on a cul-de-sac with nothing but woods behind us and a wonderful slow-moving stream on the side. We loved finding huge bullfrogs and turtles in the stream. Our neighbors were wonderful, and we became fast friends since all of us had children in the same age ranges.

I felt like my career was finally taking off. Nothing feels better than a fresh start. I had new friends and new colleagues in a new location, perfect for building on who I was as a person. I loved working, and I excelled at whatever I put my mind to. I was the first to volunteer for extra work, chalking it up to getting on-the-job training. I was rewarded for my long hours with bonuses and promotions. I started taking classes at night to get my MBA. Having a decade of on-the-job experience made me a better student this time around.

Adam and I decided to have another child. I swear I was pregnant a week after saying we would start trying. I remember coming out of the bathroom with my pregnancy test in hand. The test was positive. Adam was standing in the kitchen—all smiles.

Brendon was born on July 22, 1999, just twenty-two months after Madisson. He was born three weeks early. I didn't even have a bag packed for the hospital.

The day started with me going to work as usual, but I started to have pains in my stomach in the morning. As the day progressed, it got worse, so I called my doctor and she had me come in to check things out. After doing tests, the doctor came in and said, "We must induce labor. You need to head to the hospital right now."

"Okay, I need to run home and pack my bag first," I said.

She looked at me like I had two heads. "You need to go *now*, or you run the risk of infection and could lose the baby!" she said.

I called Adam and told him to come get me and take me to the Northside Hospital in downtown Atlanta.

When Brendon was born, he was tiny but beautiful. The hospital was busy, and I was discharged just twelve hours after giving birth. They said they would send a nurse to our home daily the first week to check on Brendon and me. Off we went with our twelve-hour-old son and a jaundice machine. I had stayed three days when I had my daughter.

Because of the cost of childcare, Adam stayed home with the children for two years. He also watched Debra's two children, Damien and Markus. Damien was born the day before Madisson, and they were as close as two friends could be. Our two families did everything together, from camping to holidays. The kids loved our time in Georgia.

My sassy northern personality at first did not fit in among those who lived south of the Mason-Dixon Line. I worked within a four-southern-state region where names like Sweetie and Honey were just part of their vernacular.

The first time I spoke with one of my agents from South Carolina, I bit my tongue each time he said, "Well, sweetie..."

My boss suggested I learn to take such comments with a grain of salt and focus on the end goal instead of ruffling feathers. Eventually I learned to soften my approach—a little—but with very few women mentors in the upper ranks, I was told by male bosses more than once that I came across as too aggressive.

However, this friction did not slow my advancement. I started a new department for commercial vehicles called the Commercial Center of Excellence.

I went on to manage all the commercial accounts in four states. I had a team of twelve, and our unit became the model for State Farm to develop thirteen of these centers across the United States.

We set up IDLs, or Interactive Distance Learning classes, to train over 1,500 agents on commercial vehicle underwriting. I eventually took over the training team and modeled it after our commercial unit. For over a year, I drove back and forth each week between Atlanta and Birmingham due to having employees in both locations.

The ultra-conservative culture, however, wore me down, and I left to work for a grittier company.

I was hired as a general manager by the National Interstate Insurance Corporation. The company was up and coming. My role was sales and underwriting manager for a $25 million book of business. As many hours as I had put in at State Farm, I worked even longer hours for this company: twelve hours a day, six days a week. I made a lot more money, but the learning curve was much steeper. We mostly insured trucks, charter buses, and commercial vehicles.

I loved the autonomy I had. I also continued to take online classes to finish my MBA. The time away from home spent working and studying began to take a toll on my marriage. With every new class I took for my MBA, we grew further and further apart.

When I was offered a marketing manager position in the home office in Richfield, Ohio, with a large pay increase, I jumped at the chance.

At that time, Adam was working for Equifax in IT and was doing well. I did not want him to jeopardize his job and move if it was not going to work out. It was then that I first broached the subject of divorce.

"If you're asking me to choose between my marriage and my career, I will choose my marriage every time," he said.

We planned our move from Atlanta to Ohio.

In the summer of 2006, I moved a few months early into a corporate apartment in Richfield, Ohio, so Adam could get the house in Atlanta ready for sale. Equifax decided that after we moved, he could work from home.

It was all coming together, although I ended up sitting and watching the Fourth of July fireworks alone from my office window.

I again wondered if it was all worth it.

We found our home in Macedonia, Ohio. Living in the secondary snowbelt of Ohio, I was often just plain cold. Though we were only a few hours from my family in Michigan, we rarely saw them.

At the kids' new school, I became the president of the Parent-Teacher Association (PTA). My kids were six and eight years old when I asked my husband for a divorce. The more time we spent together, the more I realized how lonely I was.

He was a wonderful father; we just weren't communicating anymore, so after thirteen years of marriage, I moved out.

Adam didn't want the divorce, so we tried therapy. During the first session, the therapist asked him what his dreams were.

"Whatever hers are," he said.

We never returned. I just didn't have it in me to dream for the both of us.

I also learned that the company I worked for had a vastly different idea of how women should dress and behave in the workplace. As one of only a handful of women executives, I was eventually fired for not fitting in. What the company didn't know was I had been keeping a journal of all the times I was sexually harassed—all the different times my boss had asked me for sex. Back then, women couldn't report sexual harassment, or we would jeopardize future advancement opportunities because of our "sensitivity."

Armed with my performance appraisals and my journal, I hired a civil rights attorney, and we settled out of court.

A few months later, I received a call from a broker I had worked with while at National Interstate. They needed someone to head up marketing for their wholesale division, called KF&B. They were located right outside of Los Angeles. The call came from Jeff McAnany, the vice president of sales, while he was at a bus convention in Las Vegas.

"I'm at this convention, and we have no marketing person here representing our wholesale division. Would you be interested?"

"Absolutely," I said.

Within a week, I was flown to California to interview. At dinner, the CEO of the company said, "We heard you had some issues with your other company. How do we know you won't sue us?"

It seemed odd that he knew of my situation even though I had signed a nondisclosure agreement and was not supposed to talk about it.

"Are you planning on sexually harassing me?" I asked.

"Not at all," was his response.

"Then we have no issues to worry about, right?" I said.

With that, I became their vice president of marketing. Since my territory was nationwide, I was able to work from wherever I wanted to call home.

I needed a change of scenery again, both in weather and in friends. I had gotten my divorce, but Adam and I had agreed to remain amicable for the children. We both hated Ohio. We had been divorced for three years when the kids talked their father into agreeing to move with me to Florida.

In 2011, we found Cape Coral. For work, I traveled extensively around the United States. I went with our brokers to help close the larger accounts, typically over a million dollars in premiums. On one trip to Minnesota, I was visiting a few of my larger agents. I had an agent at a large brokerage whom I had not met in person, so I stopped by his office and offered to take his team to dinner. The dinner was uneventful as we sat chatting, getting to know each other. The agent drove with me to the restaurant as it was north of his office and my hotel.

On the way back to his office, he sexually assaulted me.

I reported it to the police and my CEO; however, given I lived in Florida, the district attorney did not want to pursue charges. My CEO gave the agent's book of business to my boss. The experience made me wary of traveling to other agents' offices, but it didn't stop me from dreaming big.

The city sent out quarterly newsletters to every resident, and sometimes I would read them, sometimes not. I had left the October 2012 newsletter on my coffee table for a few weeks. I'm not sure why I had saved this particular one, but I finally picked it up and began to flip through it one evening. Midway through I saw a heading that read, "City Council Elections to Be Held in November 2013."

I had lived in Cape Coral for less than two years. I served as vice president of the PTO for the city-owned municipal charter school that both of my children attended. I did not know a woman had never occupied the mayoral seat before.

There were contests for three council seats and the mayor's office. I sat back and thought, what if I ran for city council?

I googled the locations of the districts and the qualifications to run. Each person was elected at-large, meaning registered voters within the city limits could vote for them regardless of the district they lived in; however, the seats were also staggered, which meant there was an election every two years.

To run for the seat, you had to physically live in that district for at least one year. I called my best friend Vanessa to get her thoughts as I continued to look up the district maps. Vanessa was serving as our PTO president and had become an extremely close friend and confidant. As soon as I told her what I was thinking, and before I could even finish my full sentence, she said, "Girl! You would totally rock that!"

Vanessa always had a way of making anything we did fun and exciting. From selling Yankee candles for a fundraiser to hosting teacher appreciation days, if V was involved, it was not going to be the usual humdrum event. I have always loved that about her. As we continued to chat, I located the district map online.

"Crap!" I said.

"What?" Vanessa asked.

"I don't live in any of the districts up for election," I said. "But the mayor seat is for anyone," I continued.

Vanessa agreed I should go big or go home.

The more we discussed the possibility, the more excited I became. I had not felt that excited or enthusiastic about anything since high school when I ran for secretary of our class and won. For the first time in a long time, I felt alive again. Something about being able to effect substantial change had ignited a passion in me that I hadn't felt in over twenty years.

I love people, love meeting new people, and love change even more. In my corporate life, *change* was a dreaded word.

To implement even the smallest improvement, there had to be hundreds of hours of discussion. We as management would take every scenario and beat it to death, often deciding on something that fell far short of what we were trying to accomplish.

Sitting in those corporate meetings, listening to other managers make excuses about why something wouldn't work without even trying it, used to make me want to pull my hair out.

I had never felt like I truly belonged in that environment.

Suddenly, just thinking about running for an elected position made me want to get out of bed again. I craved work that allowed me to be my authentic self. Little did I know how much this adventure would impact my lifelong passion to serve.

CHAPTER 3

THE PRIMARY ELECTION

There is no passion to be found playing small—in settling for a life that is less than the one you are capable of living. —Nelson Mandela

My interest in politics ignited when I joined the PTA of my children's school. My daughter had been diagnosed with ADHD in first grade. She had a reading disability, so I sent both of our children to the municipally owned charter school called Oasis. By year two, I was elected to the PTA board. For two years I was the secretary, and for one year the vice president. When I decided to run for mayor, I pulled strength from the other parents in the PTA. During the football season, Vanessa, my dear friend who was also the PTA president, held cookouts during which the men hung outside watching the football game and drinking their beer, while the women sat inside drinking wine and laughing about the typical things women talk about.

One evening after the game ended, the women moved outside. For a few weeks, I had been tossing around the idea of running for mayor to my girlfriends, but this was the first time the husbands heard of my intent.

"You can't win," said one husband.

The other men started to snicker.

"Yep, there's no way you can beat Sullivan," said another. "I've known him for years."

They were only the first of many to tell me that. As they continued to tease, I felt my anger growing. It wasn't the first time I had been told I couldn't do something. In fact, my entire life, I had taken immense pride in accomplishing things people said I couldn't do.

When I first told my mother I was thinking of running, her comment was, "Don't you think you should start with a smaller office?"

"No," was my answer.

Fortunately, I didn't listen to her.

As the men continued to comment, Lou Traverna, who lived half the year in Cape Coral and half in New Jersey, asked me why I wanted to run. The more we chatted, the more excited we both got while the rest of the men continued talking about football. I told him I had no idea how to run a campaign and noted that I would learn from the torrent of information on the internet.

"I'll have to learn as I go along," I said, "but my background in marketing will prove useful."

Lou suggested I hold a listening party to better understand the issues facing the city. We held a cookout at my house, and about thirty people attended, many of whom were city employees. Most signed on to volunteer for my campaign. The PTO wives brought along their pooh-poohing husbands even though the men didn't take me seriously.

I became increasingly excited as the group discussed the issues, which were wide-ranging, and the solutions, which were complicated.

Following the meeting, Lou suggested I speak with one of his friends about becoming my campaign manager.

That was when I met Janis Keim, a retired Parks and Recreation supervisor. She had worked for the city of Cape Coral for almost twenty-seven years. She was a blond, hip, Jewish woman who had moved here in 1970 and pretty much taught the entire city how to swim. Janis had just gone through a devastating divorce, and I loved her from the first time I met her. She was blunt and didn't mince words—much like me.

With her circle of acquaintances and her outspoken nature, I knew right away she would be perfect to manage my campaign. With a little nudging, she agreed. Janis became one of my most trusted confidants over the next year. She was amazingly good at campaigning.

Having grown up in a highly political home, I had sworn off ever being in politics as vehemently as my children do today. I watched my mother run for office throughout the years, even walked door-to-door with her passing out her literature. She believed very strongly that if you see something you don't like, you have the power to change it.

And so I made my first attempt at political office.

From the moment I read the newsletter announcing the deadline to qualify for the upcoming election, I knew I would run. I also knew I would win. Many people have asked me what my motivation was for wanting to be mayor, and my answer is always the same: to make a difference.

I began meeting with prominent members of the community to understand Cape Coral's volatile political past. I always ended the meetings with "Thank you! Can you give me the names of two other people I should meet with? And preferably one of those people should disagree with your views."

One of the first couples I met with was Ed Prince, the president of the Civics Association and a city employee, and his wife Linda. We met at a restaurant called Jimbo's one Saturday afternoon. They were the most adorable couple. Having met in West Virginia during ninth grade, they had wed at age nineteen and been married for almost forty years.

Ed knew everything about the city as well as the players behind the scenes. When we finished our meeting, he said, "We are behind you no matter what. It would have to take something big to sway our vote."

Both became dear friends and mentors during the campaign. Sadly, we lost Ed to cancer just a few years into my term. It still feels like there's a hole in my heart when I think of him. He was an incredible man, mentor, husband, father, and friend.

When I first announced I was running for mayor, I met with former mayor Joe Mazurkiewicz. Curiosity, I am certain, is why he met with me.

We sat at a Beef O'Brady's having lunch. The meeting with Joe started awkwardly, but after an hour of conversation, I could tell he was intrigued by my candidacy.

Joe told me he was supporting another candidate, Vince Cummings, who was a member of Leadership Cape Coral, a Chamber of Commerce program. Joe was the head of the program. Vince was a chaplain in the army and had been collecting donations from Republicans and Democrats alike since before I entered the race. The General Employees' Union, which is made up of four different unions within the city, was supporting Cummings as well and had helped him secure large donations from state union associations.

I met with Wally Ilczyszyn, the president of the General Employees' Union as well as the state Painters' Union. He was called Wally the Wrench. He looked at my business card and said in his best Jersey accent, "A woman? I ain't votin' for no woman."

The Police Union and the General Employees' Union decided not to endorse a candidate until after the primary. Prior to making an endorsement, each union gave the candidates a questionnaire to complete. The fire department interviewed every candidate who returned one.

From the moment I interviewed with the Fire Union PAC, I felt comfortable with them. They had a past record of being rebels, so it was a natural fit. They had mounted a campaign to get their previous fire chief retired by putting up a billboard that said Wanted: New Fire Chief. They even gave away bumper stickers.

I could tell when I sat down with them to interview that they were surprised by my answers. That was the first time I met Lieutenant Ken Retzer, vice president of their local fire union and chair of its political action committee.

That night I received a friend request on Facebook from Ken. We then talked on the phone for about three hours. Two days later, Ken called to inform me that his PAC had decided to endorse me during the primary, something it had never done before.

"We think it's about time a woman takes the reins," he said.

I was doing my best to keep my composure, but quietly I was jumping up and down, screaming on the inside. The endorsement sent the other unions into a tailspin.

After the announcement, you could feel the tension in the air between the unions. They did not like being forced into a corner on who to support, and the stakes were too high for them to screw it up.

Shortly after the fire endorsement was announced, I received a cryptic call from a resident advising me to attend a secret meeting. Members of the police and general union would be at this meeting, but no one from the fire department had been invited. I had no idea what this meeting was about, and I asked Ken to send someone from his firefighters' union.

I could see everyone's surprise when he and a firefighter named Jerry Doviak walked in with me. The energy in the room shifted. The meeting, as I would soon discover, was a gathering of a group of residents who were big into the political scene. The purpose of the meeting was to grill me on every topic they could think of as a way of punishing me for being endorsed by the fire department without their approval.

In hindsight, I'm glad I was a newbie to the city because walking into that house with a group of about fifty people I didn't know could have been intimidating. Luckily for me, I didn't have time to think too much about it. I noted that Wally the Wrench was not in the room while the rest of them were throwing questions at me. He was sitting outside on the lanai, smoking his cigar like he was the Godfather.

Convincing Republicans to vote for me even though I was a woman and a Democrat was not easy.

Michel Doherty, who was in her late nineties, was the grand dame of the Lee County Republicans. I first met her at a primary debate being held at the Yacht Club. I reached out to shake her hand, and with a look of disgust on her face, she said to me, "You will never win with that hair. It is not professional."

She turned and walked off.

Chastised, I cut my hair to look more conservative, and after the primary election she came around to support my campaign.

Cape Coral had a history of far-right-leaning groups taking hold of the elections, but after Trump was elected, they were even more energized. There was a sudden electricity that spilled out as our city council and school board members were pushed further and further to the right.

Right-wingers were railing against gun control measures and started bullying elected officials to change local ordinances to fit the far-right narrative.

I needed support to push back against the far-right groups, and one who helped me was former council member Alex LePera. She and her late husband had been part of the fabric of Cape Coral's politics. She was a Democrat and had a strong base of friends who worked alongside her during elections. Alex had lost her daughter to suicide, and she often told me how much I reminded her of her daughter.

Between Michel Doherty on the Republican side and Alex for the Democrats, I found it much easier to maneuver through the political landscape. They were both brilliant and each offered me advice on the best way to handle situations that arose.

Michel taught me about people, elected officials in particular, and showed me how to discuss policies in a way that made them take action. She knew when a policy topic would be an issue with her party. She would walk me through how to address their concerns so we could pass ordinances. I was usually able to cut off any potential issues before they could make a big deal about it, which often meant tabling the discussion.

She also never hesitated to come forward at a city council meeting to discuss a controversial topic or to support me.

When the city was proposing a Domestic Partner Registry that afforded certain rights and benefits to qualified long-term, committed relationships that were registered with the City of Cape Coral, Michel came to speak in support of the registry, wearing her beautiful red silk scarf. She knew the Republican Party was against gay marriage and this ordinance, so she made it known how she felt. The party never said a word and the ordinance passed.

Alex, having been on the city council in the past, knew the city employees. She talked me through policy changes and discussed the best ways to communicate my requests to the city manager to gain his support. She had a talent for anticipating how changes would affect city employees and relating their concerns in a way everyone could understand. She was also a brilliant negotiator.

The campaign was on, and I was fearless as I walked into events, including ones in enemy territory. I was not fazed even when one nasty resident, referred to as the Witch of Bergen County, stood outside our events passing out misinformation about my past.

Since I was a Democrat, I was not allowed to participate in Republican candidate debates. The first big Republican debate was held at a local bar. Since I couldn't participate, my team thought it would be fun to show up anyway, wearing our

Team Marni T-shirts. There were about thirty of us, and we took up one whole side of the room.

One man kept walking by me, calling me names. Ken quietly walked over to him and leaned in to say a few words. I never found out what he said, but the man left me alone for the rest of the evening.

Before walking into any campaign event, debate, or meeting, I would listen to my power songs to get in the right frame of mind. My theme song became "To Fly" by Nicki Minaj, featuring Rihanna. The lyrics fit perfectly, not only with my experience campaigning but with my entire term as mayor:

> I came to win, to fight, to conquer, to thrive
> I came to win, to survive, to prosper, to rise
> To fly
> To fly

The Republican Party decided to hold a second debate at a military museum within the city. This time the debate was open to all candidates. Everyone, and I do mean everyone, told me not to go. Most were sure I was being set up.

I went anyway. I figured that if I was able to change even one voter's mind, it would be worth it. From the moment I walked in, people kept coming up to me, saying things to knock me off my game. Their statements were passive-aggressive, like "Aren't you worried tonight with so many

Republicans in the room?" or "I'd be so nervous if I were you." They would add a smirk.

When the debate started, we were each instructed to ask one question of any of our opponents. All four of the other candidates directed their one question to me. A candidate who claimed he had found a shipwreck in the canal near his home asked, "Is it Miss or Ms.?"

"Doesn't matter," I replied.

"Are you a homeowner?" he asked.

I smiled.

"I've owned three, built one," I said. "Since my divorce, I don't have a honey for my honey-do list, and I hate fixin' anything, so no, I don't own."

Some of the women in the audience snickered.

While I may have looked fearless answering questions, I couldn't wait for the debate to be over.

Joe, the former mayor and chairperson of the Chamber of Commerce, told me I needed to raise a minimum of $85,000 to even be a threat to the incumbent. As a Democrat in a Republican city, I knew I wouldn't be able to raise that amount of money, but for many years I had been accustomed to being underestimated as a woman in corporate America, so I knew it was just a matter of outworking my opponents.

Many times, I had been underestimated in the workplace.

I remember one time, while at State Farm, I asked my manager how I could move up to our corporate office in Bloomington, Illinois.

"You will need a sponsor to move up," she said, "and because no one knows what will come out of your mouth next, finding that sponsor will be difficult."

My immediate response to that slight was to send out my resume, and within two weeks, I was offered another job making 30 percent more than I was paid at State Farm.

I had been campaigning for five months for the primary and had only ten weeks to get my message out for the general election. It didn't take long before the Republican Party put out its first negative mailer. Members of Mayor Sullivan's team created emails disparaging me. They sent out postcards calling me a liberal as though it was a dirty word. My yard signs, which were not cheap to make, kept getting stolen, and my large signs that I had placed near major intersections were getting run over in the middle of the night.

My team was worried that my opponent had the means to create a commercial to air against me on TV and cable. Such a commercial cost around $5,000, and I didn't have the money to do the same.

A few weeks prior to the election, I made a call to Brendan Fonock, the fire department president, to see if he had any fundraising ideas.

That night as I ate dinner, I received a notification on my cell phone. "You received $25."

Then another. "You received $50."

I sat in disbelief as one notification after another came in. Brendan had sent a statewide text message to every firefighter asking for my help. Overnight, I raised enough money for the commercial.

Wishing to run an admirable campaign, I refused to allow my staff to send out even one negative mailing. I was so proud of the positive campaign we conducted.

From the very beginning, our campaign was different. First, it was staffed by mostly women. Second, we worked hard at going into the community to speak with as many people as we could. The usual strategy is to make phone calls, but with cell phones becoming the norm, you could make fifty calls before talking to a voter. Going to many kinds of events gave you instant access to the voters.

We held listening parties. Many of our fundraisers were intimate gatherings where supporters gave whatever they could afford.

Having their names listed as donors was more important to me than getting large sums of money from them.

"It's important for our list of donors to showcase the diversity of the group supporting our campaign, and we want that list to be long," I often told my team.

Making the evening more special was the fact that much of my campaign team had never been active in politics before. Most of my volunteers had not been motivated to work on a campaign until this one.

I have always been able to energize and motivate people to make changes. People in the community called us the Blond Brigade because a large majority of my team was blond.

I am sure in the beginning it was not meant as a compliment, but after we won the primary, we were seen as a force to be reckoned with.

Janis Keim and Olympia Sasso, who were now *both* heading up my campaign, were amazing. Like Janis, Olympia had worked for the city in the Parks and Recreation department. In one of our meetings, volunteers were worried we would not be able to get our message out without a large amount of campaign funds.

When it came to deciding which events to attend, my team decided to shake things up a bit. Instead of meeting with the same groups as the Chamber of Commerce over and over, we agreed to attend any event or meeting where five or more people congregated. We split up the events and made sure we had people handing out campaign literature at as many events as possible. From the farmer's markets to the New Residents Club, we covered a lot of ground.

We also ran an incredibly effective social media campaign, which was a key component of winning the election. I met with over 250 residents and virtually every group or club within our city. Understanding that raising money would be difficult, I knew I would just have to outwork the others. Not until early voting did my opponents finally realize that I was a threat.

MS. MAYOR

Two of my opponents, A. J. Boyd and David Carr, combined forces and began passing out "Wanted" posters to everyone walking in to vote at the election office. The poster

they designed had a picture of Sharon Davies, a prominent Democrat, and me side by side. In one corner there was a rainbow, and in the other was a marijuana leaf.

I can laugh at it now, but at the time, it was devastating. In hindsight, their portrayal of me as a pot-smoking lesbian helped gain me a few extra votes. That and I had great hair in the picture. Two of my opponents in the Cape Coral mayoral race passed out the flier.

My volunteers stood on virtually every busy intersection waving signs and wearing T-shirts that said Team Marni. Even their dogs sported shirts. The fire department held a cookout the week of early voting at the election office and put my extra-large Marni for Mayor signs on wood frames. They drove the big signs around in the back of pickup trucks. At the same time, I tried to be in as many places as I could, shaking hands and asking for votes.

I wasn't surprised by the outcome. I somehow knew I would win both the primary and the general elections.

With six candidates vying for the seat of mayor in the primary, Sullivan took 37 percent of the vote, and I took 22 percent.

My opponents were all men: Alan "A. J." Boyd was a former council member, longtime resident, and realtor. He got a late start in the election but still came in with 19 percent of the vote. Dan Ashby, a military man with a son who was disabled in the Gulf War, garnered 12 percent of the vote. Vince Cummings, who was supported by the General Employees' Union and Chamber of Commerce, took only 8 percent, and finally David Carr, a Democrat who entered the race at the last minute with close ties to the incumbent mayor, took less than 2 percent.

Now that I had won both elections, my enemies could move on to more important issues: a recount and who I was dating.

CHAPTER 4

DATING WHILE IN OFFICE

Your task is not to seek love, but merely to seek and find all the barriers within yourself that you have built against it. —Rumi

As I walked up to the fire department union hall for my candidate interview, I was not nervous at all. To prepare for the interview, their president, Brendan Fonock, had answered my questions as I studied the issues facing their department.

When I walked into the room, there were six men sitting around a table. The vice president of the union and chairman of the political action committee was named Lieutenant Ken Retzer. His friends called him Kenny. He went last in the introductions.

During the interview, they asked me questions about their pension plan and pay. I gravitated to Ken as he spoke. He commanded the room, and I could tell by how the others spoke to him that he was respected.

Near the end of the interview, one of the men asked me, "Do you promise to work with us on anything we bring to you?"

"The only promise I will make," I said, "is that I will always be fair and will always tell you where I stand on any issue."

They nodded. I could tell from their faces that I had impressed them, but I had no idea whether they would endorse me.

"We will be making our announcement on July 31," Ken said.

After the interview wrapped up, Ken walked me to my car. I got a better look at him. He was tall and rugged looking with salt-and-pepper hair. I liked him immediately. He certainly had a swagger to him, and he was not wearing a wedding band. He lingered at my car and chatted for a few minutes before I left. As I pulled away, I couldn't help but be a little intrigued by him.

That evening, I received a message request on Facebook from Ken. I figured he was doing his due diligence and checking on my social media profile. When I messaged him back, he asked if he could call me. Of course I said yes.

We talked for hours about everything: our ex-spouses, kids, and careers. Talking to him was easy. We kept the conversation focused on general details of our lives, but I could tell by the way he spoke that he was interested in me. Our banter was quick-witted. I didn't hear from him again until July 31, the day they made their decision about who to endorse.

When the phone rang, I picked it up immediately.

"Good afternoon, Marni. This is Ken Retzer calling from Local 2424," he said. He sounded so formal with his southern drawl.

"Hey! How are you, Ken?" I said.

"We have made a decision on who we are endorsing," he said.

You could hear a pin drop on my end as I sat there in anticipation.

"We think it's about time for a woman to take the reins of the city. We've decided to endorse you to be our next mayor."

"Thank you, Ken! I won't let you down!" I said.

I was jumping up and down in my kitchen in total disbelief. He went on to explain that the firemen had never endorsed anyone in the primary but felt I would need the leg up considering I was so new to the political scene. Ken also said that he would like to attend a couple of my campaign meetings to get a feel for my volunteers and the structure of my campaign. He talked about how active he had been in the two most recent elections.

Toward the end of the conversation, Ken asked, "Would you want to meet tonight for a celebratory drink?"

I agreed almost immediately.

That evening we met in downtown Fort Myers at a local Irish bar. When I walked into the bar, he was sitting at a corner table to the left. From the beginning, the conversation was easy. This time we talked about more personal things like being divorced, our children, and the last time we had dated someone. He told me he hadn't dated anyone in a long time. I hadn't either.

There was never a quiet moment between us. We ended up talking until the bar closed. As he walked me to my car, we kept talking. He got in on the passenger side and we continued talking for another hour. Before he got out of the car, he leaned over and kissed me goodnight. There was so much chemistry between us.

I had never had this kind of chemistry with anyone before.

From then on, I called him Kenny, and he continued to call me every day. A week later, he attended a campaign meeting at my home. My volunteers were excited to have him there, considering he had so much experience in campaigning. As the meeting got started, it seemed a little chaotic. I could see the concern on his face as people continued to talk. He chimed in a little, but mostly he observed.

After the meeting, he stayed until everyone else had left, then turned to me and said, "Okay, that meeting was a hot mess!"

"It wasn't that bad," I replied.

"Everyone was talking over each other, and it was hard to follow," he said.

"Don't worry," I said. "Everyone has their part to play, and while it may seem chaotic to you, it's working just like I want it to."

Just as I finished my sentence, he walked over and kissed me.

I could feel the kiss from my head to my toes.

He continued attending my campaign meetings and we spoke every night for a month.

Then suddenly it stopped.

We went from talking every day to only a few days a week. He was distant, but I didn't know why. I didn't have the time to think too hard about it, so I just kept moving forward with campaigning. I had enough on my plate without having to wonder why he didn't seem interested anymore. Weeks went by, and the majority of our discussions were centered around specific campaign issues. He was engaged in my campaign; he just didn't ask me out anymore.

Two weeks after I received the fire union endorsement, I had my construction industry PAC interview. Brian Rist was the chairperson of the PAC. When the interview was complete, Brian asked if I would come to his office because he had additional questions for me.

I met him and his CFO at his company to discuss my campaign platform. He was the owner of Storm Smart, a local hurricane shutter manufacturer. He was average height with dark hair. If I had to guess at the time, I would have said he was ten to fifteen years older than me. He had lived in Cape Coral for over eighteen years and knew who was who in the city. He gave me a tour of his place, and afterward his CFO joined us in his office to talk some more.

Brian was also the chairperson of the Cape Coral Construction Industry Association (CCCIA) as well as the Southwest Regional Manufacturing Association. Because my specialty as a consultant was strategic planning, he was interested in discussing some of the issues he was facing as a business owner.

After I took the tour, he asked me what I thought his biggest challenge was. I asked him how he knew which product was the most profitable. He didn't have an inventory system in place, and with as many as seven change orders happening for numerous jobs, I wondered how he knew what the company's true profitability was.

He was sitting at his desk, looking at me in the chair in front of it with amusement on his face. We began to talk at length about my education and background.

After an hour or so, he leaned back in his chair and placed his hands on the back of his head. Smiling, he said, "I can't believe I'm about to say this."

"What's that?" I asked.

His smile grew. "I've never voted for a Democrat, let alone donated to one."

"And that means what?" I asked.

"It means I'm donating and voting for a Democrat for the first time with you."

I smiled.

After a few minutes of chatting, I held my hand out and said, "So how much are you donating?"

He laughed aloud. "What's the contribution limit?" he asked.

"Fifteen hundred per person or entity," I said.

With that, he took out his checkbook and wrote me a check for $1,500.

Brian then asked me to work for him as a consultant, putting in a new inventory system. We finalized my contract in August right before the primary election.

I started meeting with his managers the following week in preparation for putting together his strategic plan. In October, he told me he had moved into the Westin Hotel. He was separating from his wife of over twenty-five years.

Brian said she was abusive and drank a lot. She hit him in his sleep and accused him of being with other women. I knew he had left her several times before but always went back. This time, he said, it would be different.

I told him I would support him any way I could. We had become friends. There was nothing we couldn't talk about. Though my being a Democrat intrigued him, we found out we had similar beliefs, and I enjoyed our banter.

After I began consulting for Storm Smart, the local manufacturing association was looking for a new executive director. I interviewed with the board. Brian abstained from voting because I was already working with him.

The board hired me, and I was ready to take on the new task of rebuilding the association. A few people raised concerns to the media about my hire; however, everything was legitimate, so I didn't worry too much about it.

Brian was excited that I had won the primary election. Because I was having a difficult time getting larger donations as a Democrat, he decided to give me a donation from each of his companies, along with a personal donation for the general election. I was grateful for his support.

I received the CCCIA endorsement as well. Brian was a great person to help me prepare for debates. Between him and Kenny, I honed my platform, and my confidence grew.

As I worked with Brian, I heard from Kenny only when he wanted to discuss the campaign or any rumors he had heard. The night of the general election, once I was announced the winner, Kenny left the party with his union brothers to go congratulate the other winners on the city council. I did not see him for the rest of the evening. Brian, on the other hand, sat and chatted with my parents for hours. However, it was not until Thanksgiving that Brian and I had our first date.

I have always considered myself an open book on pretty much everything. It never occurred to me that people would be interested in whom I dated.

Looking back, I see that was foolish on my part and very naïve. While I did go on dates, I rarely took anyone with me to events. Nothing was ever said to me directly; however, I just did not want the headache of explaining why the person I took to one event was not going to the next. Before Brian and I started to date, I had only one request. I never wanted to have a conflict of interest with him on the dais. He agreed.

He hadn't worked with the city for over three years. The city had purchased storm shutters from his company in the past, and his company performed maintenance on them from time to time, but that was it.

When I was invited to the Seminar for Newly Elected Mayors at Harvard University in early December, I took Brian with me. His ability to talk to the other mayors and speakers was amazing. As CEO of his own company for years, he was comfortable in this setting. He got to sit in on my seminar, and we spent hours talking about the mechanics of my being in office.

Storm Smart had a location in Cancún, Mexico. Brian asked me to go with him to Cancún over Thanksgiving to go through the operations down there.

We were focused on how we could include this location in his inventory system. I met his partner, José, for the first time in Cancún, and it was there that he asked me and my kids to move in with him.

He had rented a condominium at Cape Harbor overlooking the Caloosahatchee River. We moved into his place in January, though I kept my rental unit. I liked having a quiet place to go when things got too hectic. He filed his legal separation papers in early December and his attorney gave us the green light to move in together without jeopardizing his divorce case. I didn't know that his wife had hired a private investigator to watch us both.

The kids adored Brian. They loved his condominium as well. He took the three of us to Saint Maarten for the holidays. It was there that he bought me my first piece of jewelry—a large diamond promise ring. It was gorgeous.

I asked my attorney if I needed to put the ring on my financial disclosure for the quarter. He said no. There is a provision in the law that if a gift is from family or a boyfriend that I intended to marry, I didn't have to disclose it. The statute was very broad.

Brian, the kids, and I had a wonderful time taking in the local atmosphere. New Year's Eve was fabulous. It was hard getting on the plane to go back to Cape Coral. I was still tired from campaigning and now the recount was getting underway.

I adored Brian, though I didn't have the kind of connection I felt with Kenny.

In February 2014, Brian and I were on our way to the airport to go to Jamaica for my birthday when I received a call from Kenny. We didn't talk for but a minute, but I could tell from the tone of his voice he was upset when I told him I wouldn't be back for a week. I told him I would call him when I returned. He called me a couple more times while I was in Jamaica, but we spoke only briefly.

The day I returned, Kenny wanted to see me but wouldn't tell me why. I agreed to meet him anyway. He asked me to come out to his house in Alva. Something deep down told me not to go, but because he had basically disappeared, out of curiosity, I went.

He was extremely upset that I was with Brian.

"Dammit, Marni, I love you," he said with tears in his eyes.

"I'm dating Brian," I said. "I haven't heard from you in months. What do you want from me?"

"I'm not ready to date yet, but I don't want you to date him either," he said.

"Well, that isn't going to happen. I'm living with Brian now," I said.

The conversation just kept going around and around until I finally got up and left.

Once the sting of that conversation subsided, we were able to remain friends. I would go fishing with him from time to time. He didn't ask about Brian, nor did we talk about anyone he might have been dating.

I loved how I felt when I was with Kenny. Being able to disappear into the vast waters of the gulf without anyone recognizing me became my retreat. It felt like our friendship had existed forever. Still, I didn't allow myself to get too caught up in my own feelings for him.

In June 2014, Brian bought us a huge home in southwest cape on the Spreader Canal.

He surprised me one day by stopping at Brian Gomer's office to discuss the house that had just gone up for sale. I loved the home, so he told Brian we wanted it. The home had two stories with a beautiful view of the spreader canal. There was a natural preserve directly behind us. It had an infinity pool that looked like it dropped off into the canal and two primary bedrooms downstairs.

My daughter felt like a princess in the second primary suite. My son had his room upstairs complete with a huge TV for him to play his video games. He also had a private balcony overlooking the water. We put a hammock on the balcony so he could sit outside and enjoy the view. We also built a boat dock, and for Christmas, Brian got each of the kids a wave runner.

For Christmas, we decided to surprise the kids and my parents with a trip to Italy. None of them had ever been to Europe, and with the stress of the recount, we all needed a break from Cape Coral. Brian had his travel agent pick a few places to stay, and he worked with my mother to choose the home we ultimately stayed in.

Brian had graduated from the University of Massachusetts and set up an endowment program through the school. Every time the board of directors came down to visit, he loved showing off that he was dating the mayor of the city. It was a trade-off for all the events I took him to.

In January 2015, I was invited to the inauguration of reelected Republican governor Rick Scott. Councilwoman Rana Erbrick was deep into the Republican Party. She had started a new local chapter of Women Leaning Right. She later used this group to help her with her bid for mayor, though I didn't know about any of this at the time.

I asked Rana if she wanted to attend with me. She was excited to go and agreed immediately. We drove in my car to Tallahassee. This was one of the last times we would get along.

During the trip, I told her about Brian and me. She asked about the ring I was wearing. It was a beautiful chocolate diamond LeVian ring that Brian had given to me for Christmas. Brian, who was kind and generous, had given me his gas card for his company and I used it to put gas in my car during the trip.

The trip was fun, and we got to meet with our elected state officials. Even though I was a Democrat, no one seemed to question why I was there. I promised myself that I would work with whoever was in office, Republican or Democrat. It was the right thing to do for the residents of my city.

We stayed only one night and were back home the following evening.

Brian was busy with his business and couldn't go. There was nothing he wanted me to discuss with the governor. Given the size of his business, Governor Scott often came to see Brian with his entourage to tout his new jobs program.

I enjoyed decorating our new home. The kids had their friends over to swim. We had a long firepit that ran the length of the pool, and the kids loved hanging out around it. Brian and I hosted parties for our friends.

He traveled with me to various conventions, and I continued working on the inventory system for his company.

The two of us could discuss just about anything. We were together when the 2016 presidential election between Donald Trump and Hillary Clinton was gearing up. He was a staunch Republican, so I often teased him that our votes would cancel each other out.

At this point, I had been in office for over a year, and Brian and I could really see how people might perceive a situation in contrast to what was really happening. Decisions were never made in a vacuum at the local level, and though Donald Trump and Hillary Clinton were so far apart on most issues, Brian and I were able to meet in the middle most times, which was refreshing, considering the noise of the election and the discord that was bubbling up.

Brian loved buying me unique gifts for my birthday, Mother's Day, and Christmas. He said he had bought his ex-wife jewelry, but she rarely wore it. Every time we traveled, he would surprise me with a new pendant or earrings. He was one of the most generous men I had ever met.

He went out of his way to make me feel beautiful.

While I loved Brian and the life we were starting, I couldn't help that I was falling in love with Kenny. I considered him one of my best friends and confidants. Being that he was closer to my age, there was more chemistry between us than with Brian.

I knew I should have cut off contact, but something kept me wanting to be close to him, even if we were just friends. However, I was determined to make it work with Brian.

Valuing Brian's business for the divorce was taking forever, and it was becoming clear that he would have to pay his ex-wife a hefty sum of money—a little over $5 million to be exact, plus alimony, the house, and a Porsche.

As time went on, Brian was getting more agitated. His wife had never worked, so he felt that she didn't deserve half of the business. He had built it from the ground up, and with no children between them, he was determined to fight to the end to keep what he felt was his.

The tension began to take its toll on our relationship to the point that it felt like we could never really move forward. There were times his wife would show up drunk at our new home, yelling. She made it clear that she was not interested in a divorce and was going to do everything in her power to keep him.

The more she persisted, the more it pushed me away.

I started talking to Kenny more each day.

In that Brian's divorce had not yet been resolved, most of the things we bought were in his name only. To help alleviate my concern about not owning anything, we looked for a condominium I could purchase.

Our goal was to have a place for our family to stay when they came to the cape to visit. We wanted it to be in my name; however, I was having a tough time getting a mortgage because my consulting business was relatively new and my mayoral position was an elected one. Brian agreed to pay cash for the condominium, but we drew up a contract between us.

I gave him a down payment of $36,000 and would make payments until I could get a mortgage of my own.

One night things came to a head for Brian and me. I was on the phone talking to the assistant city manager when Brian started pacing around the room. As I looked up at him, he was tapping his finger on his watch. I paused my conversation to ask, "What's wrong?"

"You've been on the phone for over an hour with another man while in my house," he said.

His remarks took me by surprise. *His* house. Was that how he referred to our home? He had always told me it was *our* home. Along with not moving fast enough, I felt we weren't building a relationship that was on a solid footing.

I hung up the phone and snapped back. "You are absolutely right! This is *your* house, not mine."

I had taken a leap by dating him. I was not used to relying on anyone, but I didn't make anywhere near the money he made.

For the first time in our relationship, he had made me feel like I was trapped. In the heat of the moment, I yelled, "We'll be moving out tomorrow!"

"Fine!" he replied.

I know he didn't think I was serious.

The house I was renting had only a month left on the lease. Rather than move back there, I decided to move into the condominium. It made better financial sense than having to make a rental payment and also pay monthly for the condominium.

The very next day, I hired two men to come and move our belongings.

I needed space. When Kenny found out I was moving, he offered his truck to move the furnishings from my rental to the new condominium. I didn't tell Kenny that I was purchasing the condominium and paying Brian monthly for it. I wasn't sure how he would react to it, which should have been my first clue that the relationship we were starting wasn't necessarily a healthy one.

I loved how Kenny made me feel. We started hanging out more, and he gradually began staying over."

Although Kenny and I had intense chemistry, we also had intense arguments. At first they were just disagreements that seemed harmless. But I soon saw that he was grooming me to gauge my tolerance. I can describe how I felt only by comparing myself to a frog placed in a pot of hot water that was slowly beginning to boil. The frog does not realize he's boiling to death until it's too late.

Kenny began love-bombing me almost immediately after we had an argument. He'd buy me gifts, give me cards, and text me beautiful quotes.

I began getting a funny feeling in my gut whenever he spoke of Kirsten Thompson, a politically active member of the community and his former girlfriend. They had been working together for a while and she had been instrumental in pulling together data for his union to present to the city manager.

I had never realized how often they talked on the phone. He knew I how I felt when they talked, but he would try to assuage my feelings by saying they were just friends. Even though I knew their friendship had gone back to at least 2009, I tried not to give in to my feelings of doubt.

By December 2015, Kenny and I were dating. He asked me to go to his union Christmas party. It was a great evening. I even got to know Kirsten better. She was seated at our table next to me and had come by herself.

There were highs and lows in Kenny's and my relationship. In the beginning, the highs were amazing, but over time the lows became too tough to overlook. For example, one year I asked him to visit my family in Michigan over Christmas and New Year's. As the trip became imminent, Kenny began to get moodier. On our flight to Michigan, I was tense because I had not always been on the best terms with my parents. We were staying at my best friend Amber's home, but I was still anxious about his meeting my family. He started getting upset with me, saying I was overreacting. By the time the plane set down, we weren't speaking to each other.

It was late when we finally got our rental car and headed to my friend's home. Not much was said during the car ride.

When he was upset, he often said passive-aggressive things to me or didn't speak to me at all.

That Christmas was the last time I was genuinely happy with Kenny.

Back home in Florida, I was getting ready to attend the US Conference of Mayors in Washington, DC.

Kenny became more and more agitated that I was traveling so much for my political office. By the end of January, we were arguing often. He had always been intense in text messages or voicemail. Now a lever had been switched, and he became even more intense.

There was so much going on at that time. I was working extended hours on our water quality issues. He didn't like the amount of time I was spending with Mayor Kevin Ruane of Sanibel, and he continued to rail against Brian.

To me, the past was the past, but Kenny did not see it that way. While working, I would not respond to his obsessive texts or voicemails. Every argument took hours to overcome, often going late into the evening as we went round and round. My sleep was being disrupted, and I was becoming more exhausted by the day.

While I was at my conference in Washington, a huge snowstorm hit the area and my flight home was canceled. I had to spend hours looking for an alternative way home. I ended up taking an Uber to Richmond, where I rented a car, then drove from Richmond to Cape Coral.

Kenny was irate. I had not been accessible to him during my trip, and my flight cancellation took him over the edge. As I drove through the night, he continued to leave me voicemails and send angry text messages. I did not have the energy to deal with them, so I turned my phone off for most of the trip. When I finally turned my phone back on, his voicemails began to worry me. I had heard him yell before, but these messages were over the top.

"You don't have one minute to do anything, and I think that's bullshit," he said in one of his voicemails. "What it comes down to is if you don't think you can do your job and be in love with me, well, then that's something you got in your mind that doesn't make sense to me. If you want to talk, then pick up the phone," he said forcefully.

I was tired and responded, "I don't think we should be together."

He did not agree.

When I returned home, he showed up at my condominium to rehash our differences once again. I loved him, but it seemed I couldn't make him happy. Until I did. He could change his demeanor in a second's notice.

We ended up reconciling once again. For my birthday in mid-February, he surprised me with dinner after our council meeting at Nevermind Restaurant. My council, city manager, and his wife were present along with some friends of mine. The city manager, his wife, and our city attorney incredibly shared the same birthday as me.

The following weekend, Kenny and I went out for dinner and drinks at a local restaurant. It turned into a nightclub after 9:00 p.m. He'd had too much to drink and began getting belligerent with anyone who approached me. Embarrassed by his outbursts, I asked him if we could leave.

"Let's go!" he said.

On our way to my car, he continued to yell at me in the parking lot. I walked faster, hoping no one recognized me. Social media was already hard to read, and I did not want our drama to make any headlines.

We were about halfway to my condominium when he said, "Let me out!"

"No. Let's just wait until we get home, and we can talk," I said.

"Let me out!" he screamed.

I pulled over to the side of the road and he got out, slamming the passenger side door. He started walking. I drove slowly next to him with my window down.

"Get in, Kenny!" I pleaded.

He lit a cigarette and kept walking. After a few minutes, I pulled away and headed home. He came walking in about twenty minutes later, angry. We argued for the rest of the evening, until I told him, "I don't want to see you anymore."

"If that's what you want, fine!" he said as he walked out the door.

For the next two months, our relationship was strained, but we continued to talk, though not the way we used to.

I could feel a change in him, but I didn't know what it was. He seemed distant again. Luckily, I was busy. Work kept my mind off our relationship issues. What I didn't know was that he had started talking to Kirsten again. He also started telling her and her friends things about me that weren't true. Eager to get me out of the picture, they obliged him. In May, he called my mother and met with my ex-husband to gather information about me. My mother didn't share all that they had discussed about me. Whatever it was, she had riled him up. My ex-husband, Adam, didn't help the situation either.

After Kenny spoke to my mother and Adam, I started to get cryptic messages from him telling me, "I had no idea how corrupt you were."

"What are you talking about?" I said.

"You know what you've done, and you're in some deep shit, Marni. You need to get out while you still can."

Working as the mayor full-time as well as doing my consulting work, I was exhausted. I didn't know what he was talking about, so I decided to ignore him and not get involved. He could be a lot to deal with emotionally at times.

I later came to regret this decision.

CHAPTER 5

OPPONENTS DEMAND RECOUNTS

Show me someone who has done something worthwhile, and I'll show you someone who has overcome adversity. —Lou Holtz

Cartoon in the *News-Press* the day after the General Election.

Though I won the election for mayor on November 5, I wasn't sworn into office until November 18, 2013. In the interim, I was what they call the mayor-elect.

Until the actual swearing in, the incumbent mayor still acted in his capacity. It's a very awkward stage in the political process because those who did not vote for me did not yet consider me mayor.

In previous years, outgoing elected officials cleared their offices out almost immediately, allowing the successor to move in. The incumbent also held handoff meetings with the mayor-elect to discuss the issues he was working on to help with a smooth transition.

John Sullivan did none of that. He carried on as if he was going to continue to be mayor while his political cronies were working on a fruitless lawsuit to force a recount.

Every year, Cape Coral has a large Veterans Day parade honoring our American heroes, paying tribute to those who have lost their lives and those who are currently serving our country. Most elected officials ride in a convertible or on a float. However, I decided to walk with my children the entire length of the parade route. Newly elected council member Richard Leon walked with us.

I asked the grand marshal, a big Sullivan supporter, where we were supposed to be in the parade.

He ignored me.

I asked him again where we should go.

"I don't give a damn where you go," he said.

He turned around and walked away. Linda Biondi, a kind woman who had organized the parade, came over to show us where we were to stand.

In one of his last official duties, Sullivan rode in the parade along with other outgoing council members.

As my children and I walked the parade route, I paused frequently to shake hands and wave at cheering supporters.

Whenever a concentrated group of Sullivan supporters was gathered, we would hear loud boos, but we were so overwhelmed by the number of people that the slights were easy to brush off.

Veterans Parade in Cape Coral, Florida, on November 11, 2013.

I wanted to ask Sullivan about the nuts and bolts of being mayor. Were there any hints he could give me as I began my term in office?

Sullivan refused to meet with me.

I would have to figure out the mechanics of the job as I went along.

The headline of the November 15, 2013, *Cape Coral Breeze* read "Sullivan to Contest Mayoral Election Results."

The following day I was served court documents. Sullivan and five of his supporters alleged in their lawsuit that "certain inconsistencies and irregularities occurred which resulted in Marni Lin Sawicki being reported as the successful candidate and winning the election by the Election Canvassing Board."

There had been no inconsistencies or irregularities. These guys just couldn't stand the fact that they had lost the election to a woman and had to give up their reign of power.

David Carr, the Democratic challenger in the primary election for mayor, was one of the plaintiffs. Other plaintiffs were staunch conservative Lisa Cohen; former council member Bill Deile, who was also a member of the Cape Coral Minutemen and Road Ahead Gang; and Steven Crane.

It was the first time a losing candidate had contested an election in Cape Coral's history. We would make history many times over. The suit contended there was misconduct by election officials, problems with signatures on absentee and mail-in ballots, and defects in the voting system. (This might sound familiar to those of you who follow national politics today.)

Among those listed as defendants were Lee County Supervisor of Elections Sharon Harrington, Council Member Rana Erbrick, City Clerk Rebecca Van Deutekom, and me. They filed suits against me individually and in my official capacity as mayor, requiring me to hire two separate attorneys. The city hired its attorneys to represent us in our official capacity. I did not have the money to hire my own private attorney, but Allison Tant, a representative of the state Democratic Party, called to tell me they were sending Mark Herron, a well-known Tallahassee-based election lawyer, to represent me. Mark was the lawyer who took the Republican Party to the Supreme Court for gerrymandering in 2012 and won.

The judge shot down Sullivan's request for a recount, but she granted him an unofficial ballot inspection, which he and his group had to pay for.

On the day of the trial, Sullivan's attorney pushed for a revote and then asked for an entirely new election. He argued that I could not have possibly had such a huge lead in the early voting, but not on Election Day.

It was a flawed argument in that the majority of Democrats sent in mail-in ballots, and Republicans usually voted on Election Day. The same thing had happened in the presidential election of 2020, when Joe Biden received the majority of the mail-in votes and Donald Trump got the most votes on Election Day. Trump too could not figure out why Biden had such a huge early lead.

The argument was bogus, and the judge saw right through it. She awarded attorney fees to the defendants. Sullivan and his gang were required to pay for court fees amounting to almost $250,000.

After the decision, I wrote on social media, "And yes . . . I am Mayor!" which immediately sent my critics into a tailspin. Sullivan, who, like Trump, refused to accept that he had lost, filed an appeal.

Sullivan lost his appeal the following June, and in July we went to mediation to determine the exact cost of our legal fees. In October, the city council decided not to sue Sullivan for the entire amount of the attorney fees, and he agreed to pay $125,000 including court costs. Mark Herron agreed to amend his fees and received $48,000, while Sharon Harrington, supervisor of elections, received $77,000.

Almost one year from the date when I was elected, the election dispute saga was finally over.

I was sworn in on November 18, 2013. My childhood best friend Amber Purchis flew down from Michigan to swear me in. But from the beginning, no matter what I did, someone was there to criticize.

My mentor Alex Lepera chastised me for wearing a black dress to the swearing in. "You look like you're going to a funeral," she said.

The swearing-in ceremony. *Left to right:* Amber Purchis, Brendon Sawicki, Madisson Sawicki, Marni Sawicki, Janis Keim.

As I stood in front of the dais with my left hand on the Bible and my right hand raised, I looked over at my smiling children standing next to me. Seeing their proud faces made the fierceness of the campaign worth it. I was teaching them about resiliency and winning graciously. I was teaching them that they can do anything they put their minds to.

Janis held the Bible for me. As soon as the swearing in was over, there was a short recess, and then I sat down in the chair, once the domain of John Sullivan, as the new mayor of Cape Coral.

I was grateful for my experience with running meetings and using Robert's Rules as an officer of the PTA and PTO. My first council meeting went smoothly.

We were off!

Even though I knew the statistics about how large Cape Coral was, it didn't register until I received an invitation to attend the Seminar for Newly Elected Mayors at the Harvard Institute of Politics in Boston in early December 2013. The invitation went out to a small number of mayors who were elected in cities with a population over 75,000 and was held in conjunction with the US Conference of Mayors organization.

Around forty newly elected mayors were selected to participate, and I was one of them. Other mayors who attended were Rick Kriseman from Saint Petersburg, Florida, and Nan Whaley of Dayton, Ohio, who had been chosen as the first woman Democratic nominee for the Ohio gubernatorial race. Phillip Levine from Miami Beach was also invited. He went on to run, unsuccessfully, for governor of Florida in 2019. Also present were Marty Welsh, who is currently serving as President Biden's labor secretary; Howard Wiggs of Lakeland; Buddy Dyer of Orlando; and Bill Paduto of Pittsburgh.

The entire experience was surreal. Harvard brought in former mayors, police chiefs, and other leaders to show newly elected mayors how to get things done. We had dinner at the

John F. Kennedy Museum and toured the private Kennedy quarters at the museum.

I learned that to enact a new project initiative, I had to have shovels in the ground by year two or the next election cycle would wreak havoc on getting it completed. Candidates used these initiatives to draw out voters either for or against the project. The seminar gave me the running head start I needed to succeed in this new position.

My city council immediately voted to join the US Conference of Mayors. In the past, as previously stated, the Republican leadership had preferred to keep Cape Coral isolated and insulated, turning down both state and federal money and assistance. Their policy was backward and against the best interests of our city. Things were about to change in Cape Coral.

Under my administration, Cape Coral was finally taking a seat at the table and taking advantage of state and federal policies. The following January, in 2014, I attended my first conference in Washington. A group of about 150 mayors was invited to the White House to meet President Obama and Vice President Biden. The meeting was held in the East Wing.

I left the White House a huge supporter after hearing President Obama speak in person. He was warm and kind from the moment he walked into the room. I was sitting in the front row with Mayor William Capote of Palm Bay, Florida. When President Obama opened the room for questions, the mayor of a town in Minnesota stood.

"Okay... so first, I think you're awesome!" she said. Before she could finish her comment, Obama paused her.

"Wait. Wait. What? Hold on. I don't often get to hear praise, so can we stop for a minute and just bask in my awesomeness?" he said as he put his hand to his chin, pondering the moment with a slight smile. The whole room broke out into laughter, even the Republicans.

President Obama and me.

As the event wrapped up, Obama and Biden walked down the front aisle shaking our hands.

"Can I take a selfie?" I asked the president.

Obama laughed and said, "If I take one with you, I will have to take one with every mayor here, and I will never leave."

I turned my camera and took one anyway.

It was at this conference that I realized just how big Cape Coral was. The sessions were broken down by city population: one session for mayors of cities under 50,000 people, another for mayors with a population of 50,000 to 100,000, and finally a third session for mayors with city populations over 100,000. Cape Coral's population was well over 100,000. As of 2020, it had 203,000 residents.

There was a metal detector for one of the lines, the line for mayors of cities over 100,000. Behind me was Mayor Bill de Blasio of New York City. We moved through the line quickly, and I took my seat somewhere in the middle of the room.

With a look of confusion, someone leaned over and asked what city I represented.

"Cape Coral, Florida."

"Are you sure you're supposed to be here?"

"This is for cities with a population of over 100,000, correct?" I said.

"Yes," the person said.

"Then I'm in the right place."

I was in complete amazement that the mayors in my presence represented cities such as Seattle, Houston, Boston, New York, and Dallas.

Before I took office, no one even knew where Cape Coral was. I vowed I would go on to change that.

In May 2014, I was invited to a workshop by the Mayors' Institute on City Design in coordination with the Endowment for the Arts. The weeklong workshop was held in San Antonio, Texas. The group consisted of seven mayors and some of the best urban planners in the country. I wanted this talented group to assist me with a project I hoped to get off the ground in our city.

The project, called Bimini Basin, would redefine our city and give us that gathering place I so desperately wanted for Cape Coral. Mitchell Silver, the past president of the American Planners Association and former urban planner for Charlotte, North Carolina, agreed to take a good look at my project.

As I stood to present our project, he interjected. "You mean you live on the coast of Florida surrounded by water, with over four hundred miles of canals in your city, and your downtown has no water as a focal point?" he asked.

I sighed, and replied, "Yes."

"That's never going to work," he said. "You must move your downtown to your Bimini Basin area."

After the meeting, I was put in touch with the director of the University of South Florida (USF) architectural department. She agreed to produce three distinctive design options for my project. In addition, she and her department would charge only $50,000 although typically designing a project like that would cost almost half a million dollars.

I was extremely fortunate to have been offered this help. Mitchell Silver went on to serve as the parks commissioner in New York City under Mayor de Blasio.

After returning from the Mayors' Institute of City Design trip, I knew my city council would need convincing to move the Bimini Basin project along, so I met with various groups in town and spoke about what our downtown could be. With their buy-in, I asked someone from each group to come to the next council meeting and show support for the project.

Council members Rana Erbrick and Richard Leon, who were trying to make names for themselves in the Republican Party, disagreed with anything and everything I brought up on the dais.

Rana was championing another project called the Seven Islands. She contended that the city would be unable to do both.

Her issue was not that the city could not do both. Her issue was that I was the one bringing forward the Bimini Basin project. She was already working behind the scenes to run for mayor in the next election.

She had to differentiate herself from me, and opposing this project was her way of doing just that. Councilman Leon was just young enough that Rana could use his naivete to her advantage. The two of them met secretly. I knew this because someone from the fire department had sent me a photo of them sitting together at a restaurant.

In Florida, the Sunshine Law forbids elected officials on the same board from meeting in private to discuss something they might vote on. All discussion and project work by council members must be done during an advertised council meeting. I knew their meetings were illegal, but there wasn't much I could do about them.

Various groups came to the council meeting to support my project, and my council voted to approve bringing the USF architects in to create three visions of what the Bimini Basin would look like.

Rana wasn't happy, but there wasn't much she could do.

USF students came down and gathered input from as many residents as they could, then hosted community meetings to go over their presentations.

We were presented with three viable options for building our new downtown.

Designing the Bimini Basin project was the easy part. The hard part was convincing the part of the community that wanted our city to remain a sleepy bedroom community. They had all kinds of complaints:

"The canals will carry the music from the area to my house."

"Drunk people will be on the roads."

"Traffic will be horrible."

And on and on.

I can't take credit for coming up with the term *CAVE people*—Citizens against Virtually Everything.

Mayor Sly James from Kansas City had coined the phrase at one of the mayors' conferences I attended. Yes, that did seem to fit some of the citizens of my city. As elected officials, we always heard from the unhappy minority. Residents who were happy kept silent and lived lives of contentment.

Cape Coral consistently voted out those who tried to breathe life into the city. This turnover made it difficult to get anything done within the city limits.

A few characters were perpetual complainers. Given that our term as elected officials lasted four years, the complainers who impeded growth learned quickly that all they had to do was outlast the elected official they opposed. Wait four years, and they might have a new one who believed as they did.

The project moved along, and we voted to hire a project manager to explore potential interest among developers. After we met with our county commissioners about the project, they were excited too. And yet I will never forget what one of them said to me.

His name was Larry Kiker, and he was the liaison to the group called Six Mayors of Lee County.

"I think it's great you're working so hard to get this project in," he said. "Your city needs it; however, I hope you're prepared to never see it done while you're seated as mayor."

"Why is that?" I asked.

"Because you'll do all the messy work of getting everyone used to the idea and pushing it forward, but it will take the next couple of mayors to finish it, and if they move it forward, they'll get the credit."

"It's right for our city, Larry."

He agreed.

I met with a construction/project expert in our county named Bob Koenig to have him explain private-public partnerships, or P3s, to me. If we were going to get this project off the ground, we would need the private sector's expertise and financial assistance.

I also attended a Mayors Mean Business forum, where I met the attorney who had written the P3 statute for Florida. The city eventually brought him in as a consultant to help facilitate the project.

At one of the homeowners association meetings, a group of residents complained about the project. They did not want it for a multitude of reasons.

"Will everyone who does not agree with the Bimini Basin project please raise your hands?" I said.

Most of the people raised their hands.

"Okay, I need each of you to take out your checkbooks and write a check for an additional fifteen hundred dollars in city taxes," I said.

The grumbling was loud.

"If you don't want to pay extra in city taxes to help build out this city, then you support my project," I said. "You can't have it both ways. I personally want other people, meaning snowbirds, to pay for our growth. That means gas tax, sales tax, bridge tolls, bed tax. If we had a destination place for people to visit, all these taxes and tolls would increase, giving our city the additional money we need to continue building it out."

I was surprised how many understood what I was saying and came around to my point of view.

The newly elected mayors seminar I attended had said that as soon as the next election came up, candidates would come out of the woodwork to rail against the project, and that's exactly what happened. I left office with the project manager in place, but it would be up to the next group on the city council to continue moving the project forward. I have no doubt the Bimini Basin will be completed. The question is just how long it will take.

Although working in corporate America had taught me about emotional intelligence and I had learned to be self-aware when I was discussing sensitive issues with my employees, when I became mayor, I was often surprised at the topics that would trigger residents' anger.

This happened to me early in my term, when council member Richard Leon brought forward a resolution on behalf of a group of residents regarding the Second Amendment and gun rights. These residents wanted to make certain their local leaders would not allow their guns to be taken away.

In local government, a resolution is just an affirmation, whereas an ordinance changes the law.

The resolution was brought forward at a time when gun laws were being debated nationally. When the resolution made it to our agenda, the council chambers were filled with people who turned out to support it.

Tallahassee had just passed an ordinance banning guns from its city limits. The problem was that every council person takes an oath when sworn in to protect and uphold all the amendments in the Constitution. This resolution wanted us to reaffirm we would protect the Second Amendment, and it included a paragraph that was sharply critical of President Barack Obama.

It was one part reaffirmation, one part "We hate the president."

Many residents guessed correctly that we would not support their position, and public debate became extremely emotional. Each speaker had three minutes at the podium to address the council, and in an effort to support the resolution, they threatened, yelled, and cursed at us while other audience members cheered them on.

Prior to the debate, I should have called a recess to calm emotions, but I did not.

As we began the discussion of the gun resolution, we on the council couldn't get two or three sentences out without people from the audience blurting out obscenities. No matter what any of us said to explain our reasoning, no one would hear it.

We as elected officials swear under oath to uphold the entire Constitution. Doing so made the resolution redundant.

It has often been said that when emotion is high, intelligence is low. This was certainly the case. We denied the resolution, but the residents who brought it forward only heard "We support taking away your guns."

They did not pay any attention to the logic behind the decision. Though they claimed the resolution was made to unify our community, it accomplished the opposite.

We rejected the resolution by a vote of six to two. Our rejection of a promise not to take away their guns, even though no one was taking their guns in the first place, caused those who had proposed the resolution to flood our inboxes with emails of contempt. They demanded we do our job and reconsider the vote.

If diplomacy does not work first, they figured, contempt and calling into question our patriotism was sure to do the trick. As political science professor Peter Bergerson said to the local *News-Press*, "It purely would have a symbolic value as opposed to any legal precedents or any legal authority. It sounds like it is really not well thought through and perhaps self-serving."

Self-serving described many residents' motives throughout my four years as mayor.

The Second Amendment group was led by a resident named Lisa Cohen, who was a devoted member of the Republican Party. She was also a plaintiff in the lawsuit demanding the mayoral recount.

Shortly after I was elected, I attended a school board meeting with House Representative Heather Fitzenhagen and fellow council member and educator Derrek Donnell.

The school board was preparing to opt out of the Common Core curriculum, which details what K–12 students throughout the United States should know in English language arts and mathematics at the conclusion of each school grade. The National Governors Association and Council of Chief State School Officers sponsored the initiative. Common Core was passed in forty-four of the fifty states, but many Republicans hated the idea the same way they hated and fought the Affordable Care Act. These Republicans disliked the federal government dictating *anything* to state governments.

The problem with turning it down was that our schools would lose thousands of dollars in federal funding. Since I had a daughter with ADHD and a reading disability, I was fully aware of how that lack of funding would affect her. She would lose funding for additional learning resources and tests that would determine her progress, which could set her back years.

I approached the podium to speak to the school board and discussed my daughter's disability.

"If you want to opt out of Common Core, please do it when you have a contingency game plan," I told them.

Heather and Derrek both discussed the need to keep federal and state funding in place. The board meeting was televised.

Lisa Cohen did not care about my feelings or the feelings of my daughter. Like most Republicans who opposed me, she fought dirty when she didn't get her way. Despicably she video-clipped the part of me talking about my daughter and plastered it all over social media with a quote saying, "She's as stupid as her mom."

Fox News picked up the story and started airing it on the eleven o'clock news.

The next morning, I went into my daughter's room to wake her before she went to school. It was heart-wrenching. I sat down on her bed and said, "Madisson, honey, I need to talk to you about something."

She sat up in her bed and wiped the sleep from her eyes.

"Fox News is airing a story about me going to the school board meeting yesterday, and they're talking about your disability," I said. "You don't have to go to school today if you don't want."

Her response was perfect.

"I don't care, Mom," she said. "I do have a disability, and they can kiss my ass!"

I laughed aloud as I hugged her.

"I love you, and every day you amaze me," I said. "Don't ever stop being strong."

With that, she got out of bed and went to school, and we never discussed it again. I filed a cease-and-desist order against Lisa Cohen. She later used the order to continue bolstering her case against me.

I learned a valuable lesson. I had given her a platform to reach her supporters. If you don't respond to your haters, I discovered, eventually they get tired of talking to themselves.

This was a lesson I had to learn repeatedly throughout my time in office.

Meanwhile, my issues with Kenny were escalating.

CHAPTER 6

THE RESTRAINING ORDER

Most of the shadows of this life are caused by standing in one's own sunshine. —Ralph Waldo Emerson

On May 16, 2016, Kevin Ruane, the mayor of Sanibel, his resource director James, and I attended the Fort Myers Beach council meeting to discuss our water quality efforts. Sanibel had many activists living on the beach, and the collective message from elected officials was not consistent. We hoped we could unite our cities. The meeting was scheduled for midafternoon, and I had been receiving threatening texts and phone calls from Kenny through much of the morning. We had broken up a week before. In fact, while Kevin, James, and I were sitting in a side room preparing for the meeting, I was doing my best to hold myself together, but it was obvious I was distracted as my phone continued to light up every time a text or a call came in.

"You need to hear what I have to say before it's too late," Kenny was saying. "There are people gunning for you, Marni."

I became visibly upset, and both Kevin and James asked me if I was okay. I wiped my eyes and told them I had some personal issues going on.

My personal issues became increasingly troublesome as the hours went on and Kenny's messages began to intensify. There were hundreds of texts like these:

"Although everything that happens points to you being a bad person, I don't believe that's who you really are and refuse to believe that."

And "I am not trying to hurt you believe that but there are many others that are and unfortunately, they will have no problem doing so and that's not the life you want to or need to live. I am a rescuer and as a rescuer I am telling you that you need to rescue yourself before life brings you down any further."

And "I loved you Marni and cannot just give up and walk away or sit by and watch you hurt yourself or get hurt by the people and position you're in any longer. My only hope and prayer is that you take what I have said to heart. You can block me out if you want but you are not helping yourself by doing that. Right now, you need a friend. A true friend with no agenda other than you. This is some serious shit you have gotten into, and it is gonna take you being serious to get by this without any more damage to you or others."

This wasn't the first time he had sent me messages like these. Many times after we broke up and I would not respond, he sent confusing texts trying to bait me to answer him.

It usually worked, and we would get back together. But this time the breakup was so bad that I made a promise to myself to cut off all communication. It was the only way for us to be truly over.

His texts went from one extreme to the next. One minute he was calling me names, and the next he was telling me he loved me.

It was exhausting.

I texted him: "Don't ever call or text me again. You are hateful and mean and this was exactly what I was afraid of. If you keep it up and continue to harass Lynn, I will ask for a restraining order. Leave me alone and THANK YOU for making this easier by doing this."

In response his text began: "Hateful and mean coming from a lying whore doesn't mean shit to me. You should have been afraid of it. You fucking did it to yourself yet I'm the problem for telling you about your ass?

"What do you think you can fuck people over and hurt them that they don't have a say. Fuck you and fuck Lynn." After disparaging Lynn, he wrote, "A restraining order? That's chicken shit and you're chicken shit for suggesting it. Typical lying bitch that gets caught and threatens a restraining order. No need. I don't need to talk to you. I'll just let people know what a fuck you really are. You're done.

"You sure as fuck don't deserve me . . .

"You did this, not me . . .

"I didn't do this so you shouldn't expect I wouldn't fight back."

I texted back that his texts were horrid and he should stop sending them. Once again, I told him I was going to get a restraining order. I warned him not to come to my house or my office or to call or text. "You need to stop calling and harassing people."

He sent one more text message that ended, "I'm telling you I love you and I wouldn't hurt you."

I feared he wasn't going to take no for an answer.

I had become close with all the mayors in our county over the past few years. Kevin knew what I was going through, and I could see the worry on his face as tears filled my eyes. Regardless, we proceeded with the presentation at the Fort Myers Beach council meeting.

Toward the end, one of the town council members took issue with our presentation and started asking questions that appeared rude, lacking a basic understanding of what we were trying to explain.

As Kevin and James sat down, I could feel the emotion rising within me. I hadn't intended to speak, but it was as if I was on autopilot. I approached the podium and proceeded to explain to the council member that I didn't appreciate her tone. It was a short exchange and one I regretted as soon as I stood to speak; however, I was just too overwhelmed with Kenny's messages to contain my own emotions at that moment.

I left the meeting only to get in my car and see several more messages waiting for me. Of course, my interaction at this meeting made the news later that evening, prompting council member Rana Erbrick to publicly call for my resignation. At our next meeting, Rana demanded my resignation and sent emails to all our elected officials apologizing for what she called my appalling behavior.

I had my own council meeting that evening. Meanwhile, Kenny's messages were becoming increasingly agitated—more urgent and ominous. His voicemails were a mix between "If you don't answer me, you're going to get what you deserve" and "I love you, and we can work this out together. Just admit what you did."

Throughout the afternoon leading up to the meeting, he left these voicemails.

I knew I was too emotional, tired, mentally drained, and concerned for my safety to attend my own meeting that night. This was the only council meeting I missed because of Kenny.

I sent an email to my assistant letting her know I would not be at the council meeting, and within fifteen minutes Kenny called. He left a voicemail saying he knew I wasn't going to the meeting.

I hadn't responded once all day, and my mind started to race. How did he know I wasn't going? One of my council members had to have told him.

"Meet me at Bob Evans on Pine Island Road in 30 minutes or 4:30 p.m.," Kenny wrote. "Look, I do not want to see you hurt or in trouble you can't get out of. I talked to my uncle who is a police officer. He has dealt with some pretty serious shit, and you need to hear what he told me."

I felt like I was in some bad horror movie—like I was that woman walking into a situation where the audience already knows the outcome, the one who's clueless as a man comes up behind her in the dark to stab her to death.

I had no intention of meeting Kenny. I was petrified, given his erratic behavior. He had been intense before, but never to this degree. It scared me.

My phone dinged. His text said, "I am here. Are you coming?"

I didn't respond.

The next text came fifteen minutes later. "Fire department at your house doing a welfare check. Answer the door."

Again, I didn't respond. Someone started beating on my door.

"I am well. Leave me alone," I texted back.

The knocking got heavier and louder. It was Kenny, and he was yelling at me to answer the door.

Another text dinged. "Come to the door," he messaged.

"Noooooo," I wrote back.

"Stop it, Marni. Answer the door," he responded.

"Leave me alone." I wrote it again. "Leave me alone!" And again. "I'm not answering the door!"

I wrote one text after another, then called my best friend Lynn and asked her to come over.

"Then I'll have someone else come by," he texted.

"Leave me alone!!! You have done enough already. Leave me alone!!" I wrote back.

"I have not done enough already. Stop it. I'm not mad. We need to talk. I am glad you're ok," he messaged.

"I do not feel well. I'm not answering the door. People who love me are checking on me. You can go away," I replied.

"If you want to tell me to fuck off after we talk then fair enough. But you need to understand that it is not about what you've done or how I've handled it. It is about what's out there. I do not want to hurt you," he wrote.

"You already have hurt me. Hurt me to my core. Go away."

He pleaded, "You know I love you and care for you but those checking on you do not know what I have to tell you. Jesus Christ."

"I won't open the door to you," I said.

He was so intense. I got my pistol and set it on the table next to me, praying I wouldn't have to use it.

I continued, "And nothing more can you do to hurt me. Already done. Now please for the millionth time, leave me alone."

"I'm trying to help you. I don't give a shit about what's happened," he said. "That's not what this is."

I texted my girlfriend Lynn, "Please, hurry," and responded to him, "I'm not your problem anymore."

I did not feel comfortable calling the police. Besides, if I called the police, that would just add more drama to an already potentially explosive situation. And given he was a lieutenant in the fire department, I didn't trust I would be helped. Plus, the police would take a report and the media would be all over it the next day.

I couldn't take much more.

"Jesus, Marni. Meet me at Bob Evans and you can leave when you want, fair enough?" he responded.

"No. I'm not leaving this house," I replied.

"Why?" he wrote.

"I want to be left alone."

"Did you read the long text I sent you? Yes, or no?" He asked.

I wrote, "That is what you wanted. Complete isolation. Well, you won. Now leave me be."

"Did you read it?" he asked.

"Yes, and I have no idea what you're talking about and I'm in no shape to hear it," I said.

"Huh? No idea?" he replied.

I wrote, "I can't and won't take much more, Kenny. I won't."

"Look, you have to listen to me. I'll do it on your terms," he responded.

"It'll have to be some other time. I'm in no condition for this."

It felt like time was standing still. With eight straight hours of nonstop texts and phone calls, I couldn't think straight if I tried.

"I won't say a word to hurt you. We don't have time," Kenny said, which had me puzzled. Time? I was scared for my life, and he wasn't making any sense to me.

"Don't have time for what?" I replied.

"Some other time might be too late," he wrote.

Again, we hadn't spoken in a week, and nothing had happened in between, so I was lost at what he was talking about. I knew one thing: I wasn't going to answer that door, call him back, or meet him anywhere.

"Come out and say it," I wrote. "What are you referring to? I haven't done anything illegal and resent it being suggested."

"Resent?" he said. "Then call me."

"What are you suggesting I've done that you need your cop uncle involved?" I asked.

"I don't care if you meet me," he wrote. "I'm not texting it."

I replied, "We aren't meeting!"

"I know. Call me," he said.

Again, I begged for him to go. "Leave me alone. You have done enough already."

He wouldn't stop.

He said, "And my uncle is no joke. I do not know who is telling you what, but they're not telling you everything."

He kept on. "Can't hurt to call, Marni. Can only help."

And on. "You don't have to meet me or see me ever again if that's your choice, but at least talk to me."

"If you ever cared about me, or my caring about you, you need to call. It's about you saying you're going to resign and shit. There's a bigger picture here and I care what happens to you."

"Answer your phone. Jesus! I'm not trying to hurt you. We are both hurt already."

Finally, Lynn arrived at my house with my former campaign manager, Janis.

I responded, "My friends are here. Leave me alone."

Kenny continued sending me long texts as he had that morning.

"WOW. You don't have the friends you think you have. You know damn well I was your best friend. Those friends aren't going to save your ass." He continued, "Unfucking real. Your friends helped get you into this mess." Then, "Fine. Have it your way. Your friends aren't lawyers, and they are part of the problem. When the shit hits the fan, you'll see how many real friends you really have. I was your only true friend and am still trying to be, but you won't hear of it. That's your choice. You've gotten yourself into a mess not only with us but other things. I'll leave it at that. I hope you take what I'm saying seriously. This is not a game. You've hurt me but this isn't about me. It's about making sure it stops here. Reread the long text I sent you and quit taking advice from your 'friends.' "

His messages were taking on a passive-aggressive tone as they continued. "I'm trying but you're being foolish and have been. If you want to take your chances, then that's your choice ... Best bet would be what you said yesterday, which is resign, move on as much as it hurts me to say that. This city and everything else have taken its toll on you. For god's sake Marni love yourself for once."

The day before at the council meeting, I had blurted out to one of my tormentors that I would resign rather than go through more harassment.

He went on.

"And just so you know, I'm not here to debate the legalities of what's happened. And a heads up—those may be making light of it or giving you advice don't know either, but it's not always just about legal or not. There's a court of public opinion out there gunning for you; that's the heads up."

While he continued to text, I took a sedative to calm my nerves, and I went and laid down in my bedroom while my girlfriends stood guard in the other room.

I needed the momentum to stop. It was just too much.

That evening I got a four-page text.

"You're no woman's hero. If those women, the real women, knew who you really are, they would be disappointed. You had all the right tools, Marni, but you screwed it up by not being able to control yourself or hold yourself to the high standard you profess. . . . You have a chance to be a Hero. I guess it's just a matter of just how long you want to push your luck with everything you've done and you justifying to yourself and continuing your charade. You can claim innocence and play the victim, but the real victims are those that thought you represented something special or genuine. .

. . Stop trying to paint me the bad guy. . . . You need therapy like yesterday.

"Like I said, your position or convoluted ideas about life aren't healthy. Don't listen to your friends. They're not the ones that will be left suffering. They will go about their lives, and you'll be left taking the brunt. I know your insecurities, and I know being the mayor fills part of your void, but nothing is worth giving everything you have to."

Eventually, the texting stopped around 11:00 p.m.

I got up the next morning, after having time to rest and think about all that he had wrote, and texted him. Nothing was making sense, and now *he* was not responding. After not hearing from him all day, I grew even more concerned for my safety. He hadn't gone this long in over a year without texting and calling. It was almost scarier than the day before because I had no idea if he would be waiting for me when I left my house.

I decided that evening to go to court and file for an injunction in the morning.

Walking into the courthouse to obtain the injunction was difficult. I couldn't make an appointment to request one. Instead, my daughter and I went down to the courthouse at 8:00 a.m., when the court opened, to complete the paperwork and wait for the clerk to retype my statement.

By lunchtime, there were hundreds of people in the courthouse waiting room area. Since I was mayor, most of them recognized me.

I felt violated by the process. The environment was cold and uncaring. There were women in the waiting room with small children who did not speak English trying to fill out their paperwork with no help available to translate. The appointments were first come, first served, and if you didn't get in to see the advocate before 4:00 p.m., you had to come back the next day and start over. I wondered how many women never came back the next day.

I spent almost half the day at the courthouse filling out paperwork and waiting for the judge to rule. At 4:30 p.m. the judge granted me a temporary injunction and set a date for a formal hearing a week later.

With that, I left the next morning for Indianapolis to attend a training seminar on city business that was put on by Transportation of America. I had been one of six people selected from our state to learn how to measure the success of large-scale transportation projects.

I landed in Indianapolis around noon and took my phone off airplane mode to find I already had news outlets calling and leaving me voicemails about the injunction.

Someone had tipped them off.

I never felt more alone or more isolated in my life. My intuition was telling me something was brewing, but I had been cut off from speaking with anyone. Kenny had called all our friends, family, and acquaintances to tell them about the restraining order and advised them not to speak to me or else they could be in trouble.

On social media, it was a free-for-all. The less I spoke, the more people made up their own conclusions. Many conspiracy theories floated around. The biggest one was that I had filed to keep Kenny from being able to speak out against me. All of them were incorrect.

I had filed because I was scared.

A friend finally called me back, and after hearing what Kenny had told her, I began to panic. She said he had mentioned our texts to her. He had threatened before to release them, and then did it again in the last few days.

It was unimaginable for me that people were seeing the messages I had sent to the man with whom I shared everything.

I called his attorney and asked to speak with Kenny. The lawyer said the temporary restraining order made that impossible. I would not know the full extent of what was going on until months later.

As I said, as his intensity grew, I became increasingly concerned for my safety. He was threatening to release our personal text messages to the media.

I hoped my restraining order would calm the situation down.

I understand now that I was in an abusive relationship; however, that realization did not come until I was out of office. Kenny and I had been in an on-again, off-again relationship. During this particular breakup, he was trying to manipulate the narrative by telling me that "people" were coming after me for something illegal I had supposedly done. He would not elaborate via text, and I would not meet with him.

This is the cycle of abuse. There is a technical name for Kenny's behavior: *crazy-making*. An article from *Psychology Today* online perfectly sums it up.

It's "when a person sets you up to lose. You are damned if you do and damned if you don't. You are put in lose-lose situations, but too many games are being played for you to reason yourself out of it. There is no rhyme, reason, or emotional understanding with a crazy maker. Worse, when the behavior is stealthy and confusing, it becomes easy to feel crazy. It feels like you are caught in a whirlwind of chaos, with the life force being sucked from you as you are manipulated with nonstop crazy-making tactics."

It would take something drastic to finally release me from the abusive grip of this relationship.

Kenny used the time the temporary injunction was in place to begin sharing information about me with Kirsten Thompson, his former girlfriend, and anyone else who would listen.

He knew the information he was sharing was not true. There were elements of truth in his stories, such as that the people were real. But the situations weren't.

For example, he told people I was an investor in Dixie Roadhouse, which would have been a conflict of interest since I had voted to keep the bars open until 4:00 a.m. Lynn, the owner of Dixie, was a friend to whom I had loaned money.

My tormentors Kirsten Thompson, Sam Fisher, and Jessica Cosden started to meet with Kenny at his home to construct the case that I was corrupt. The proof they used to connect the dots of my corruption was farfetched.

They saw only what they wanted to see.

On the day of the hearing for the permanent injunction, I was at my attorney's office across the street from the courthouse. I was already nervous because reporters were on the steps, waiting for me to walk in.

My attorney's assistant walked in the room and said, "There are three Cape Coral council members seated on Kenny's side of the courtroom."

"What? Which ones?" I asked.

"Council members Jessica Cosden, Rana Erbrick, and Richard Leon," she replied.

I knew Kirsten was there with them. The whole situation threw me for a loop. Nothing was adding up. Why would my council members be sitting with him? It just did not make sense.

The media had been running the story of my filing for a restraining order for a full week.

I was worn down and scared, so I asked my attorney, "Can we just make him sign a letter stating he won't come within five hundred feet of me instead of going to court?"

"Yes, but the letter won't be enforceable by the courts," he said.

It was a risk I was willing to take to get out of the spotlight. My relationship with Kenny was nobody's business. If it didn't prevent me from performing my duties as mayor, no one else should have been involved.

Men who are elected officials do not have people judging them so harshly. However, as I said earlier, in the spring and summer, there's not much happening news-wise, so they chose my situation to fill the void.

Kenny signed the letter to stay away, and I dropped the restraining order. He contacted me about six weeks later, baiting me into responding to his texts. It was all he needed to open the lines of communication and reconciliation.

I discovered later that during the time we weren't speaking, he had picked up where he left off with Kirsten. She reacted with furor when Kenny again tried to make a go of it with me.

She was manipulated too. Hurt people hurt people, and that is exactly what she was—hurt. Our reconciliation didn't make sense to her or her group after Kenny had given them information to make them think I was corrupt. They were sure there had to be a more sinister reason for the change in course. They figured I must have been holding something over his head.

When Kenny and I got back together, he cut off communication with everyone he had been talking to. He insisted that we needed to wipe the slate clean and start again. That entailed not speaking to the people who had supported him during the court hearing.

"I just don't understand," I told him. "Why won't you speak to them and tell them the truth about what happened between us?"

He never came clean with me about the things he'd told them about me. I didn't know he had shared personal emails between us with them all. He also did not share with me that he had taken photos of the appraisals of the jewelry I had received from Brian Rist.

Kirsten, Jessica, Sam, Richard, and Rana began their assault on me on social media. Because I was not a member of the local hate groups, I was unaware of what was permeating the group for weeks.

The topic of domestic violence is taboo even in today's #MeToo environment. No one wanted to get involved as Kenny continued to further isolate me. To control me.

With reporters camped outside my condominium, someone from Abuse Counseling and Treatment offered to walk my dog so I wouldn't have to go outside. It was overwhelming, and it only forced me to stay with Kenny.

I was convinced it was Kenny and me against the world.

What I really needed was an intervention.

CHAPTER 7

GETTING THINGS DONE

The time is always right to do what is right. —Martin Luther King Jr.

Very early in my term as mayor, I found my voice when it came to our city's legislative agenda. I'd always been taught to do the right thing, even amid powerful blowback. With only a few months under my belt, I signed the Mayors for Freedom to Marry pledge, a statement supporting same-sex marriage that the US Conference of Mayors and the National League of Cities had put together.

Momentum was building for the Supreme Court to rule on same-sex marriage, and I knew I couldn't just sit on the sidelines. I vowed I would do all I could do in my new position to make a difference. I had no idea just how loud my voice was until I signed the pledge in early 2014.

The resolution read as follows: "Now, Therefore, be it resolved that the National League of Cities supports the full inclusion of all families in the life of our nation, with equal respect, responsibility, and protection under the law, including the freedom to marry. We support the overturning of the federal Defense of Marriage Act and oppose discriminatory constitutional amendments and other attempts to deny the freedom to marry."

Given that the resolution was titled Mayors for Freedom to Marry, I didn't ask the city council for its approval prior to signing the pledge.

When my name appeared online supporting the resolution, a few members of my council and some in the community almost lost their minds. They took to social media, news outlets, and our city council meetings to voice their opposition, demanding I remove my name from the pledge.

I refused.

I had won the mayoral election by a mere 121 votes. The incumbent had filed a recount lawsuit against me. I knew hard-right Republicans refused to acknowledge that the LGBT community even existed, and they loudly and vociferously refused to accept same-sex marriage.

Signing that pledge was going to be controversial, but I stood up anyway.

Our city council voted five to three to start a Domestic Partner Registry, which allowed civil partnerships (people not related to each other) to be registered with the city. Becoming domestic partners gave legal recognition to relationships of both same-sex couples and opposite-sex couples. Equality Florida honored the five members of my council who voted to enact the Domestic Partner Registry by giving us the Ally Award in December 2014.

On June 26, 2015, the US Supreme Court struck down all state bans on same-sex marriage, legalizing it in all fifty states and requiring states to honor out-of-state same-sex marriage licenses.

It was an amazing feeling to be on the right side of history.

As soon as the state of Florida started giving out marriage licenses to same-sex couples, my assistant Pearl Taylor and her fiancée Laurie married. I became an ordained minister and performed three ceremonies, including marrying Michel Doherty's son to his male partner. I took immense pride in witnessing these amazing couples finally being able to say, "I do."

It reinforced the fact that my voice mattered.

My first legislative session with our state elected officials was memorable. The city prepared its legislative priorities each year and presented them to our state delegation to champion during the upcoming legislative session. Each session typically ran from January through April.

Living in Florida, the biggest challenge we faced as elected officials was water quality. Southwest Florida has complained for years about the dirty, polluted water coming from Lake Okeechobee during the rainy season.

Every year, Red Tide, blue-green algae, or bacteria turned our crystal-blue water to a thick Dr. Pepper color, killing off our oyster beds and leaving dead sea creatures, including dead dolphins and manatees, to wash up on our shores.

We would pound our fists, go on TV, and give interviews about how important it was to protect our waterways. Activists would stand on our bridges with signs saying We Want Clean Water, Honk If You Want Clean Water, or any phrase they thought would catch people's attention.

Many of these activists targeted our elected officials, making them out to be the enemy. The problem was that different groups had different solutions, and the lack of unity left our elected officials with nothing but inconsistent messages and no method or money to fix the problem.

Environmentalists had their own solutions, but those solutions cost millions of dollars. The solution had to be financed in Washington.

One of the first things I did after being elected mayor of Cape Coral was meet with the mayor of Sanibel, Kevin Ruane, and his resource director James Evans to learn how my city could do its part to clean our water.

The elected officials who came before me never embraced the fact that Cape Coral was the largest city between Tampa and Miami. They spent years fighting about things like fertilizer ordinances and the cost of a marketing campaign to teach residents about the runoff effects of using those fertilizers over four hundred miles of canals.

Very few people realized the power we had because of the sheer size of our city (194,000 residents at the time). I did, and I wasn't going to sit on the sidelines knowing we could boost the message Mayor Ruane had been working so hard to promote. I met Mayor Ruane and James for the first time over breakfast at a nearby First Watch. Here, Mayor Ruane and his team spent four hours educating me on the many problems surrounding water quality and why it was so important we address them. I left the meeting having pledged to do all I could going forward to make progress.

About six months later, it was quite a surprise when I received an open letter to the Lee County mayors from Mayor Ruane calling on his fellow local mayors to do their part.

As soon as his letter hit the news, my office started to receive phone calls and emails wanting to know why I wasn't doing my job. I picked up the phone immediately and called Mayor Ruane.

"What is this open letter you sent out?" I said. "My city has been working with you since I took office, and the other mayors have been meeting with us also. You made us look like we weren't doing anything, and that's not acceptable, Kevin."

There was a pause on the other end before he began to talk.

"Are you questioning my integrity, mayor?" he said.

"I am questioning why the hell you would send a letter like this to your fellow mayors and not our county or state officials, let alone neglect to advise us you were sending it so we could discuss it," I said.

Another long pause.

"You're right," he said. "How do I fix it now?"

While Mayor Ruane could be something of a hothead, I respected his ability to take a step back and admit when he was wrong. In the positions we were in, that was not an easy task. We talked for quite a while before deciding to call an emergency meeting of the mayors of our county. We scheduled it for the following week to give us time to get our talking points together.

Everyone agreed not to talk to the media before our meeting. We wanted to make a bigger impact by uniting. Unfortunately, Mayor Henderson of Fort Myers hosted a press conference the following Sunday to discuss how he was leading the mayors' delegation to Washington to fight for clean water. He even had the newly formed group Captains for Clean Water surrounding him outside City Hall.

Henderson certainly knew how to get the publicity.

Regardless of how angry he made Kevin and me, we had to admit that we had finally found a way to get our state and federal officials to listen. Instead of just belting out "We need to change," we took a different approach.

During our emergency meeting, which was televised, we discussed many issues relating to all the cities in the county. The meeting was a success. The media saw a united group with a united message: fix our water.

Left to right: Ben Nelson, Marni Sawicki, Anita Cereda, Nick Batos, Randall Henderson, Kevin Ruane.

After the meeting, Mayor Ruane and I discussed our next steps. We knew we had to go to Washington to voice our concerns, but we were questioning how to get that message across.

"What are the economic consequences to our county when our water quality is bad?" I asked.

I could see the light bulb switch on in his head.

"Not just our county," he said. "What about the sixteen counties surrounding Lake Okeechobee affected by this?"

"How can we show the impact in dollars so the state understands how important this is?" I said.

"By figuring out how much money we're losing at the local, county, and state levels because of reduced tourism, which means less gas tax, sales tax, bed tax, tolls, et cetera," he said.

"Brilliant . . . Just brilliant," I said.

The mayors at the meeting went back to our respective cities to compile our numbers. Mayor Ruane and I reached out to the Florida League of Mayors to see if they could help us with the numbers for all the other affected cities.

It turned out that the combined dollar amount that the contaminated water was costing us was in the billions, and when we made that clear, we finally got people to start paying attention.

By framing the problem this way, we were able to get the Water Resources Development Act passed in 2014 and again in 2016. Bills promoting clean water have passed biannually ever since.

If we hadn't bridged the communication gap and showed the monetary impact dirty water was having on our state, we would not have succeeded. Without all the environmental groups joining with our local elected officials' delegation, I honestly don't think anything would have changed.

Mayor Henderson, Mayor Ruane, and I went to Washington in 2015 to meet with Republican Congressman Curt Clawson about water quality. Clawson hadn't been in office long but was highly active and outspoken about the need for clean water. Since he was a Republican, his stance on water quality surprised me.

I say that because all I had heard from my party over the years was how Republicans care more about money than they do the environment; yet here was a Republican congressman clearing his schedule to take three mayors around to every committee so we could explain our concerns. He walked us to every single meeting.

Left to right: Mayors Marni Sawicki, Kevin Ruane, and Randall Henderson with Congressman Clawson.

"I've never seen any seated congressman ever do that!" said our city's lobbyist, who was a Democrat.

It wasn't hard to see why people liked Congressman Clawson. During the second day of meetings, he and I were chatting as we walked down the long corridors of the capitol building. I looked over at him, shook my head, and said, "Dammit!"

He looked over at me. "What?" he said.

"Nothing." I paused. "I just can't believe I'm about to say this about a Republican. I paused again before continuing. "I . . . actually . . . like you," I said.

With a big smile and a southern drawl, he said, "Well, I kinda like you too!"

We both laughed.

It's amazing what can happen when you knock down the walls of what we're *supposed* to believe about others and actually make up our own minds.

On the third day of our visit to Washington, we sat with Congressman Clawson in his office. Sitting with his feet up on his desk and leaning back in his chair, he asked, "Do either of you have further political aspirations?"

He was talking to Mayor Ruane and Mayor Henderson, both Republicans.

"I mean, I am about to go against everything our political party has been preaching about climate change," he said. "If either of you have further political aspirations, tell me now, and I'll keep you out of the conversation."

Mayor Henderson spoke up first. He had been mayor of Fort Myers for years and was married to the daughter of a longtime former mayor of Fort Myers. Originally from North Carolina, he still had a deep southern accent.

"Yes. Yes, ah do have further aspirations," he said.

Congressman Clawson turned to Mayor Ruane. A lifelong Republican, Ruane is a tall, feisty Irishman with ginger hair from New York. "I come from the streets of Staten Island," he would say. He had moved to Florida just prior to Hurricane Charlie and served as mayor of Sanibel for a decade. He had been fighting for water quality since the day he stepped into office.

"It doesn't matter if I have further aspirations," he said. "I'm with you."

Curt nodded and started to speak.

It was clear to me that Congressman Clawson was interested in working with and being helped by only the two Republicans in the room.

"Hold up," I blurted out. "What about me?"

Curt looked a bit baffled. "You're a Democrat," he said with an awkward laugh.

"That's what none of you get," I said. "Yes, I'm a Democrat, and guess what? We need each other. My people stand on bridges with signs. I'm positive my people could form a human chain around the entire state of Florida in less than four hours if they wanted to! Your people want the same thing here with water quality and, in this case, are the ones we need to vote with us. We would get a hell of a lot further by embracing my people and, instead of ignoring them, letting them help."

Everyone looked puzzled.

I went on, "If we tell my fanatics what we're trying to accomplish, then they can provide you some cover," I said.

"Cover?" said Congressman Clawson.

"Yes!" I said. "They can stand on the bridge with their signs and demand we do something, and you can say to your fellow Republicans, "It's not me. My community is demanding it.' "

It was a perfect fit. It might have even sounded a bit utopian; however, I've never understood why people come at problems from one political party or the other rather than from a commonsense standpoint.

There's validity in taking a holistic approach to governing. Luckily, both the congressman and Mayor Ruane agreed. The following years, we passed more legislation and raised more federal money to clean our water than ever before. I continued to meet people from both sides of the aisle who were exactly like Congressman Clawson, politicians who were there for the right reasons, not just to benefit themselves.

There's always a downside when you're a Republican and you promote action that goes against Republican orthodoxy. Congressman Clawson won the battle, but he lost the war. He did not run for reelection.

On a separate trip to Washington, our lobbyist made an appointment with Senator Marco Rubio's office. We had tried to see him on our last visit; however, somehow he could never find a time for us to meet.

The meeting was scheduled on the same day as the Right to Life march. When we approached his office, we could see him down the hall speaking with a few Catholic bishops, so we knew he was in the building.

We were escorted into a small room near his office to wait for him. Half an hour went by, and finally a young man entered and sat down at the table.

"I'm so sorry, but the senator won't be able to make the meeting today," he said. "I'm his deputy assistant. What can we do for you, mayor?"

I looked across the table at our lobbyist and shook my head. "So, let me ask you: just how big does a city need to be for Senator Rubio to give a shit? It's obviously not two hundred thousand people, so how big do we need to be?" I said.

Both the lobbyist and Rubio's assistant looked shocked.

"If the senator isn't coming, I think we're done here," said my lobbyist.

With that, we left his office.

A year later, when Senator Rubio was running for president, he brought the six mayors of Lee County together to discuss our priorities. I was a little late to the meeting and walked in the wrong door. Rubio had his back to me, and I was facing the media as I walked in. I took my seat as the senator was speaking.

During the meeting, Rubio turned to me and said, "Mayor, I know you were upset that we never got a chance to meet while you were in DC. I'll give you my personal cell phone number so next time you can coordinate directly with me."

The meeting ended, and as he went around the table to shake hands, I stopped him.

"Can I get your cell phone number now?" I asked.

He looked surprised as he was put on the spot. He stammered for a second, but when I held out my phone and said, "You can just enter it right into my phone," he couldn't get out of it.

I just smiled as he put his number in.

Sometimes a little pushiness is a good trait for a politician. It served me well for the four years I was in office.

Cape Coral functioned under a council-manager form of government, meaning the city manager reported to the city council but oversaw the daily operation of the city. Most cities have this form of government, and it works well for many. But having a city manager run the city starts becoming an issue when the population gets to be substantial. Our city was quickly approaching 200,000 residents, and at buildout, it's expected that over 400,000 people will call Cape Coral home. It's on the fastest-growing cities list every year.

As my time in the mayor's office passed, I began to realize that the city should really consider becoming a strong mayor form of government—not because I wanted to be in full control, but because as councils came and went, the city government employees never changed. The only way to change the direction of a larger city is to have the political capital to drive it. In a strong-mayor form of government, when the mayor leaves, so do most of the people reporting to them. The new mayor can bring in an entirely new staff that will help carry out the wishes of the voters, and policies can actually change.

In a council-manager form of government, the city manager just has to wait for the council to change every two years to get their way. In addition, cities end up with employees who have been there for years refusing to make the changes requested by the new council. Right before I left office, John Szerlag told me that in his twenty-five years as city manager, I was one of the best mayors he ever worked for. I told him he was one of the best unelected politicians I had ever met.

The city manager would go to each council member and present his case for whatever he wanted prior to our council meeting, shoring up votes to make sure his idea passed. Meanwhile, because of the Sunshine Law, city council members couldn't discuss anything related to the city unless we were in a publicized meeting.

It's much more difficult to change someone's mind when you have no idea what was said to them in the first place. That's exactly what our city manager did on many occasions. However, there was one particular issue he and I agreed on: our electric company was not acting in the city's best interests.

One of the most contentious contracts we had to deal with during my term as mayor was with the Lee County Electric Cooperative (LCEC), a rural, not-for-profit electric utility that had entered into a franchise agreement with the City of Cape Coral in 1971.

The agreement was amended in 1986 and was put into effect for a term of thirty years. It was set to terminate September 30, 2016, and the city needed to determine whether we were going to renew the contract, amend the contract, or purchase the company's assets and create our own utility company. The contract had an option to purchase at the end of the thirty years.

The city had a duty to our residents to do our due diligence considering the next thirty-year contract, if executed, would be worth over $10 billion.

Our challenge was that the electric company's board of trustees, paid residents, made it clear from the very beginning of the negotiations that they weren't interested in any type of compromise.

In Florida customers are not able to choose their electric provider. The Public Utilities Commission divides the areas between Florida Light & Power, LCEC, other nonprofit cooperatives, and municipally owned utility companies.

From the very beginning, negotiations were cantankerous. The company immediately hired Chris Spiro's public relations company to create a "People for LCEC" website providing disinformation to promote LCEC's viewpoints to our residents.

One of the changes I wanted to make was to the policy that customers had to wait seven years to get equity. If a customer moved and didn't provide a new address, any unclaimed checks returned due to lack of address went back into the electric company's coffers.

The company argued that the seven-year time frame allowed it to keep rates low by keeping its borrowing costs low. In other words, it argued that it used the money to get a good interest rate when borrowing money.

Its policy was to keep customers' equity if it went unclaimed for three years after the seven-year time frame, and if it remained unclaimed, the money would be put back into the company's general equity fund.

In 2016, according to the company's financial statements, of the $38.5 million in equity from closed inactive) accounts over the seven years prior, it declared $14.5 million as unclaimed and placed it back into its general member equity fund for distribution to current members.

In its 2014 financial report, LCEC had about $340 million in accumulated equity.

Another beef I had with the electric company was that it wouldn't work with the city to install underground electrical wires, wouldn't install energy-efficient LED lights, and wouldn't light school bus stops for our students during the school year.

During a Chamber of Commerce luncheon in September 2015, Dennie Hamilton, the electric company's CEO, was the speaker. He was there to give an update on the negotiations between the city and the company regarding the new franchise agreement.

Instead, he chose to use his time to give misinformation regarding our negotiations.

One of Dennie's biggest complaints was the city's insistence that when we meet with him, we have an attorney present.

When the floor was opened to questions, I stood and said, "I'm disappointed in what you're doing because you just misinformed quite a lot of people. This is why we have the lawyers involved, because if you want to negotiate, this is *not* how to do it."

Most of their so-called negotiations were taking place through social media and other media outlets in an attempt to force us into a new contract that we weren't comfortable with and that hadn't been properly vetted.

Dennie said he didn't want to offend anyone.

"You're not offending me," I said, "but you're not accurate in what you're saying."

I then walked out of the luncheon, later telling the *News-Press* that Dennie's demeanor and false statements forced me to leave.

"I would hope that would not be," I said. "I'm trying to use a word other than *snide* when he's discussing these matters. It was misinformation meant to put us in a poor light."

Dennie was making his rounds to as many public events as he could discussing the franchise agreement negotiations, but at the same time, behind the scenes he was refusing to meet with city leadership.

He forcefully rejected any talk of us purchasing the equipment from LCEC to form our own utility company.

I was asked to speak at the Northwest Homeowners Association regarding our negotiations. The room was packed with people who wanted the city to just sign a new agreement without doing the due diligence. They were arguing that because it was a member-owned utility, the money the city was spending on attorneys was taking away from our own members' money.

I explained that without an attorney, the city was at a disadvantage in negotiations. In the back of the room Jay LaGace, a frequent critic of mine, was yelling at me, "Sign the agreement!"

I equated the situation to getting a divorce when there's a lot of money at stake. If one spouse has an attorney and the other doesn't, the likelihood of being taken advantage of is high. We were negotiating a $10 billion contract spanning the next ten years, and it was important for the city to fight hard for a fair deal.

Even though our residents technically owned shares in LCEC, if we negotiated a bad deal for the city, those same residents would pay in other ways. Our problem was that we were having trouble fighting the public disinformation campaign the company was mounting against us.

After attending a Bloomberg Philanthropies conference in New York City, I met a professor from the Wharton School of

Business named Stuart Diamond. He also taught negotiations at Harvard Law School.

Mr. Diamond was discussing his *New York Times* best-selling book *Getting More: How to Negotiate to Succeed in Work and Life*. Before writing his book, he had worked for the *New York Times*, where he won the Pulitzer Prize. He even taught US Special Operations how to negotiate with terrorists. His work also consisted of persuading three thousand farmers in the Bolivian jungle to start growing bananas instead of coca for cocaine.

I figured it couldn't hurt to ask him if he would be interested in helping us negotiate our LCEC franchise agreement after talks stalled. For the bargain price of $50,000, which really was a deal considering what he charged normally, he agreed to help us negotiate.

Mr. Diamond began talks with LCEC; however, they refused to budge in their negotiations. Rather, the company put more money into its disinformation campaign, causing many residents to come to our city council meetings demanding we stop our shenanigans and sign a new agreement as is.

In the end, even though he taught special forces how to negotiate with terrorists, he couldn't get LCEC to come to any type of agreement other than the terms they had outlined already.

Unfortunately, not even an expert negotiator could aid the city in developing a new agreement. As soon as the new mayor, Joe Coviello, took my place, he signed the agreement

LCEC had always wanted. With the stroke of a pen, the option to purchase was removed and Cape Coral lost all leverage it had with LCEC.

Bloomberg Philanthropies started a What Works city program in 2015 for cities with populations over 100,000. The What Works certification recognizes and celebrates local governments "for their exceptional use of data to inform policy and funding decisions, improve services, create operational efficiencies, and engage residents."

Here's a bit more detail: "The certification program assesses cities on their data-driven decision-making practices, such as whether they are using data to set goals and track progress, allocate funding, evaluate the effectiveness of programs, and achieve desired outcomes. These data-informed strategies enable Certified Cities to be more resilient, respond in crisis situations, increase economic mobility, protect public health, and increase resident satisfaction."

As soon as the organization opened the program for cities to apply, I sent in Cape Coral's application.

At the time, I was pushing the city to create a scorecard to make sure we were making progress in the areas necessary to grow. Every year, the city manager conducts a strategic planning session with the council. We set the priorities for the upcoming year.

My background was in strategic planning and looking at data to make decisions. During the 2015 planning session, each department presented its initiatives along with how it was going to measure the impact of its efforts. The economic development director presented for his department. One of his measurements was that he would contact five hundred businesses through email.

"What are you trying to measure?" I asked.

"It shows how many companies I'm reaching out to," he replied.

"Honestly, does it matter how many you contact? Wouldn't it be better to measure how many open and/or move to our city? I would like to see what the average wage is as well," I said.

One of the goals for our public information officer was to get our Facebook "likes" up to five thousand.

"What will that tell us?" I asked.

"What our reach is," she replied.

"But just because we have that many 'likes' doesn't mean it's doing anything to improve our communication. What about measuring how many residents volunteer for open board seats?" I asked.

The process continued one by one with each department. When the Bloomberg consultant came to meet with the city manager and me, she told us the reason we had been selected was our strategic planning session.

The organization liked that I was the mayor and was so involved with the process. The certification gave us $500,000 in consulting to help us determine a better way to show our residents where their tax dollars were going.

Afterward, Bloomberg Philanthropies asked me to come to New York for its next conference to talk about the city's experience working with the consultants. It was great recognition for our city, and I was able to bring back ideas from other cities.

Cities that don't participate lose out on valuable grants as well as federal and state funding.

Each year, the Florida League of Cities awarded the Home Rule Hero to elected officials who protected their cities' right to make laws that fit their communities. Home rule authority allows cities to set up their own system of self-government. It's a local constitution.

For example, Cape Coral brought up an ordinance to ban fracking. Once it was passed, no one could get a permit for that use. Most state legislators do not like home rule authority because it means the local government makes the rules. In the case of fracking, the following year, Republican state legislators passed legislation that allowed the state to determine where fracking can and can't be done.

They did not grandfather in our ordinance with their bill, so it voided all the work we had done to ban fracking. Several times, I went to Tallahassee to fight for home rule authority. The League awarded me two Home Rule Hero Awards in 2015 and 2016.

Participating in the legislative process is one of the most important things an elected official will do. When I ran for mayor, it was to facilitate the growth of Cape Coral and to improve the quality of life for our residents.

I am proud of all we did during my time as mayor.

CHAPTER 8

THE SCHOOL PRINCIPAL WAS A CROOK

Integrity is doing the right thing, even when no one is watching. — C. S. Lewis

Many times, change or progress has been derailed because people were stuck on an idea that someone, purposely or not, put out to create a diversion. I was always amazed at how many people fell for this, even people whom I had respected and viewed as considerably smarter than me.

I understand fear holds us back; however, I am equally amazed that no matter how much proof you give some people, nothing can change their mind. It's like they're stuck in a holding pattern or drawn like a moth to a flame. They just can't take their eyes off the light, and it blinds them from even remotely seeing how preposterous the conspiracy theory is.

Let me give an example. Each year local elected officials vote on what committees they want to be part of. There's a committee for everything, but most are for oversight. These committees can vote to make recommendations; however, ultimately the city council is the only body that makes the changes.

These committees are filled with volunteers from the community who bring various issues to the forefront so they can be addressed by the city manager or policymakers. Of the twenty different committees during the time I was in office, only two held a voting seat for the elected official.

In Cape Coral, those two were the Audit and Budget Committees.

As mayor, I had been selected to sit on both voting committees; neither role was overly exciting. Both dealt with oversight of financial numbers and of policies and procedures. Until I was mayor, the Audit Committee really just functioned in the background and few people paid close attention. However, with my background in insurance, which thrives on policies and procedures, and my time on the PTA/PTO, I knew more than the average person about the inner workings of many of these two very important city functions: the city's budget and our municipally owned charter schools.

The charter school is a nonprofit organization. Both of my children attended the school, and my son was, at the time, a senior at the high school.

During one meeting, we were discussing the charter school's financial audit, and as I was perusing the columns, I asked, "Where does the money go (mostly cash) that I pay for my kids' uniforms and extracurricular activities?"

The finance director, Vicki Bateman, was a Democrat who had won the President's Award for her time overseeing the entire student loan department under Secretary of HUD Shawn Donovan. She had retired from the federal government and taken the position with the city.

We were lucky to have her. She stated that the money went into the Internal Cash Fund and therefore was not a subject of our audit.

I asked the next logical question.

"How much is in there?"

"During the last twenty-one-month period, $1.3 million has accumulated," Vicki said.

I had taken a drink of water and almost spit it out.

"Are you kidding me?" I said. "Don't you think we should audit that?"

"Well, we have wanted to for years," she said, "but it costs almost forty-five thousand dollars for the audit. The city didn't want to have to pay that cost, and the school refuses to pay for it." She added, "When the school first formed, there was only fifty thousand in it most years. It has drastically increased over the last few years."

"Can we vote to audit that fund, please?" I said.

And so we voted to audit the Internal Cash Fund. Nothing more was said about it . . . until the findings of the audit came back.

The city council had just appropriated $100,000 to the city-owned charter school from the city budget because of its budget deficit, and it was important that we make sure the money was being spent correctly. I'll get to that in a minute.

In the arenas of politics, education, and life, we often spend so much time focusing on the noise and chaos that we miss the actual problem. We allow ourselves to get too distracted by our emotions, our own insecurities, or our deep-rooted biases to see clearly.

The first step in changing anything is to listen first, and then to define the problem correctly. If we're trying to reduce the number of teenage girls who become pregnant, it's not helpful to focus on whether having sex is morally acceptable, although that's what many do debate. Rather we must focus on educating our young people about the consequences of having unprotected sex. If we then lay out their options and give them the tools or access to exercise those options, they will be less likely to have an unwanted pregnancy.

Simply putting our heads in the sand and stating it's morally wrong will never solve the actual problem of teenage pregnancies. It's just more noise. But helping kids to understand how their choices can play out in their lives will help.

Politics works the same way.

The audit took almost nine months, and finally the findings were released to the Audit Committee members along with the school's superintendent, Nelson Stephenson, and one of the governing board members.

Although the audit contained eighteen money management issues and three of them were required to be reported to the state, I left the meeting confident we were moving in the right direction. The superintendent sent me an email after we met thanking me for my "direct and authentic" dialogue.

What happened next is why it is so important to keep your eye on the actual problem and to understand how to tune out the noise.

You could say I wasn't exceptionally good at doing these two things while in office, because thirteen days later, I received a call from a local news outlet asking for a statement regarding the superintendent's accusations that I had been intimidating him.

The reporter accused me of threatening Mr. Stephenson because he hadn't renewed the district's contract with Vicki Bateman's wife, who was a teacher at the school.

Yes, I had reached out to him after her contract was non-renewed, but it was only to ask him why he had sent form letters with his stamped signature. It seemed impersonal to me.

I emailed the governing board asking what had changed between my meeting with the superintendent and the date the news stations contacted me. I received no response, so given it was Christmastime and our last meeting before the new year, I added the charter school audit to the city council agenda.

In a discussion with the city attorney about how the charter school system was born, she referred to it as the story of Frankenstein.

"First," she said, "we didn't think Frankenstein would ever move, let alone get off the table. When it did actually get off the table, we didn't know if it would ever walk. But now we have Frankenstein running through the city with no way to stop it."

The city had created the ordinance outlining how governing board members would be chosen and how the board would operate; however, at its inception, the city council, the city manager, and the city attorney had neglected to include measures for removing a board member, or the entire board, if there were problems.

In fact, the way they'd written the ordinance had given the governing board members complete autonomy but given no oversight capabilities to anyone, including the city council. When researching the findings of the audit, I became aware that teacher turnover for the previous year was 43 percent in our STEM (science, technology, engineering, and math) program.

I love the saying that absolute power corrupts absolutely, because no one on the city council had ever questioned the charter school before. There had been a police investigation about six years prior showing its policies and procedures were weak; however, no changes had been made, and the governing board was not held accountable at that time.

This time, the governing board, the superintendent, and the principal added fuel to the fire on social media. The superintendent sent emails, text messages, and social media posts asking all parents, teachers, and students to attend this meeting to stand up for the school.

"The mayor is trying to close the schools!" wrote one school official.

Really? Close the schools? With my son as a graduating senior?

Mr. Stephenson posted a link from the *Breeze* newspaper on Facebook. The headline read, "Charter Officials Vow to Forge Ahead" regarding the audit being placed on the city council agenda. With the link he commented, "Although taking a stand comes at great personal risk, I think of this . . . as one of my favorite quotes. 'A clear and innocent conscience fears nothing.' Please share with anyone that you think would be willing to attend to help take a stand."

Parents chimed in. "I'll be there!" said one parent, and another cheered, "My clear and innocent conscience will be there!"

One of the many Cape Coral community groups on Facebook shared council member Richard Leon's post about adding the audit to the agenda at the last minute. The group moderator's headline read "UPDATE: CHARTER SCHOOL SUPERINTENDENT VS. MAYOR SAWICKI."

Leon's post was meant to cast doubt on my intentions and to rile up his base of supporters.

He wrote, "It is in my opinion that we see a destructive mayor hurting not only the image of Cape Coral but the employees of our great city." He continued, "Yes, it is important as elected officials to look for areas we can improve upon, but it is also important as elected officials that we also police our peers on council."

Police our peers? I do not remember a single other time he had ever questioned another elected official.

He ended his post with "We continue to see an overstep of our mayor and I will continue to ensure a voice is loud on council about these erroneous actions."

He posted all of this prior to knowing the findings of the school audit.

Council member Leon's social media post, along with the superintendent's, was designed to motivate supporters to attend the council meeting. Many would rightly refer to this as fearmongering.

Their efforts led to over three hundred people filling our council chambers for the meeting. The room was so packed that the fire marshal stopped letting residents in. The city had to put a TV in the waiting area for overflow residents to watch. When one resident left, another could enter.

When I opened the meeting for people to give their three minutes of public comment, a line formed at the podium and twisted around the entire back of the room. One by one, people came up to say how the "mayor is wrong" and "the superintendent is amazing" or "don't close our schools."

The meeting was a complete disaster. For almost four hours, they discussed the audit, with many hurling insults at me before leaving the podium. Public comment was prior to the council's discussion, so most of the people speaking hadn't even read the audit yet.

Before the meeting started, I texted my son to ask what time his shift ended at work.

He texted, "I'm here."

"Here? At the council meeting?" I asked.

"Yes," he replied.

I searched the room for him but couldn't see where he was sitting among the crowd. A few minutes into public comment, I saw him get up and go stand in line to speak. He was standing behind Nelson Stephenson, the superintendent. When he approached, he was calm and spoke clearly.

"My name is Brendon Sawicki," he said. "I'm a senior at Oasis High School. I am in the STEM program and have had six different biology teachers this year. I think the mayor is correct, and I also would like to know why so many teachers have left."

I had tears in my eyes. With everyone yelling at me during public input, to have my son stand up for me meant so much!

"I am so proud of you for taking part in our democracy," I texted him once he sat down.

I've always said it's not about the *who* but the *what*. What had happened was pure noise created by a group of people who wanted nothing more than to divert attention from their misconduct by claiming that I was creating a hostile work environment.

At subsequent governing board meetings beginning in January 2017, members of the board made innuendos regarding the political motives behind the conflict. The superintendent was given two votes of confidence at these meetings.

In the same meeting, the board reviewed and approved a two-year contract for employment despite the concerns and without waiting for the Internal Cash Fund audit to be released the following week. The governing board had already been made aware of the findings of the audit prior to this meeting.

The city council tasked the city manager to bring back best practices from the December 12, 2016, council meeting for the charter schools for discussion. He presented them at a workshop on Monday, April 24, 2017, advising of fifty-seven different practices that should be implemented to protect all involved, including the parents, students, school, and taxpayers.

At the end of the meeting, the council instructed the city manager to work with the governing board to decide which of the best practices should be implemented. Overall, these practices would cost over $2 million to incorporate but would safeguard the system for decades to come.

I have witnessed this scenario more times than I can count over the years (again, it takes me a while to learn new things). Here, we had a school system with a budget of almost $30 million being overseen by seven council-appointed volunteers with absolute authority. They were accountable to no one.

To put this into perspective, the size of the charter schools' budget was almost identical to that of the city's fire department, which had five subject-matter experts costing upwards of $650,000 in salaries working on its budget for over six months. In addition, these experts consistently worked with other departments, such as Finance, HR, IT, and the city manager's office, in that budgeting process prior to being scrutinized by the city council.

The *what* was the money missing from the schools and how we were going to stop it from happening again. The *who* was the superintendent pointing at the mayor as if to say, "Look over there! Not here! There!"

In the end, the heat on the governing board was strong enough that they terminated Nelson Stephenson's contract on April 4, 2017, without cause.

When he left, it was determined he had coordinated some of his personal leave with council member Cosden (she sat on the board as the city council's liaison) but never turned in his request forms to school personnel to deduct from his leave bank. And the school overpaid him by more than $5,000.

Mary Wolf ▶ Marni Sawicki, Mayor of Cape Coral
5 hrs ·

I am certainly going to miss you. You brought light to many issues in the City that needed to be addressed. Something is happening at the Charter Schools that Mr Stephenson is stepping down and now The Principal appears to be leaving in a hurry. Thank you for bringing accountability and transparency where it was much needed.

A post from a parent whose child attended Oasis High School.

The police investigation took six months to complete. Unfortunately, the investigators couldn't determine how much money had been taken from the funds due to the lack of documentation surrounding purchases and reimbursements. The city was looking to prosecute Stephenson; however, he left Florida immediately after he was terminated. The city decided not to pursue criminal charges given he no longer lived in Florida.

The audit findings were outlined at a council meeting; however, council member John Carioscia decided to announce the findings on social media. He titled his post "A Revelation of Incompetence."

He went on to say, "Those who had supported the former superintendent, still continue to support him, even though the Charter School Audit, has since vindicated our mayor and revealed a disappointing and alarming report, of our Charter School System's management or maybe I should say, lack of management.

"All our mayor ever wanted was a full accounting of our Cape Coral Charter Schools. There is no getting around it; when politicians call for any action, their opponents sit up and cry 'It's political.'"

He continued, "What we have here are violations of Florida State Law Statutes, The Florida Department of Education Chapter 8, The Charter School Operating Guide Policies, as well as the State of Florida's Record Retention Laws."

Carioscia also described what he deemed incompetence. He discussed the internal funds that had been used to purchase electronic devices. None of these devices had been tracked or tagged with any asset-tracking system, so there is no way to know whether any of them were stolen or lost.

Another violation was that credit card logs or receipts were not tracked or retained. School fundraisers started by teachers were not tracked, and money was kept in desks that were not locked. All in all, over eighteen different findings highlighted where theft could have occurred.

We live in an already supercharged world right now. We feel emotions first, then we think logically. I didn't anticipate that the superintendent of the schools would try to divert attention from himself, allowing the topic to be hijacked and my fixes to be totally derailed.

Over two years were wasted on the wrong talking points, and even after I left office and Superintendent Stephenson was terminated, the subject was never discussed in a way that allowed the city to fix the problem: how to stop money from being stolen from the school.

The issue with the charter schools had come up five years prior but never been fixed by the city council, and because they had not fully addressed it, I was confident money would again be stolen in the future. You're doomed to circle back when issues aren't completely addressed, and when you do return to them, usually the problems resurface in the form of an emergency.

I sent a memo to the new council outlining the timeline and issues. I asked them to consider changing Chapter 26, which discusses charter school oversight.

"If we do not move forward with these best practices, then this entire exercise was in vain, and we've done nothing to financially secure the future of our schools," I wrote to them. "Subsequently we are kicking the can down the road for future councils to address. It is up to council to set policy for our school system, and to create the oversight to protect both the system and the city from waste, potential theft, and misappropriation of funds. Leaving oversight to the governing board, who are council-appointed volunteers, to determine which best practices they will implement is neither prudent nor responsible."

Ironically, in 2021, just as I had predicted, the charter school came to the city council to say they didn't have enough operating reserves to take them through 2024.

Instead of implementing the best practices they discussed to make sure protective policies and procedures were put in place, the city council decided to bail out the nonprofit municipally owned charter school with $2 million a year from the general fund (taxpayer money), and they forgave the $1.5 million building lease that the school owed to the city.

No one had an appetite to go through the circus that ensued after I first brought the shortcomings to everyone's attention.

Many efforts we can all think of have focused on symptoms rather than causes. The protests over George Floyd's death at the hands of the police is just one example. Rather than have the tough conversations or, more importantly, put the blame on the wrongdoer, people deflect. It's important to get ahead of these conversations from the very beginning and continue bringing people back to the underlying problem to be fixed. It's not an easy task, but it is a critical one.

While I was rather good at handling conflict, this experience showed me I still had a lot to learn.

CHAPTER 9

GETTING MARRIED

To love is to burn, to be on fire. —Jane Austen

Over the years, Mayor Kevin Ruane of Sanibel and I became close friends. We had spent a lot of time together traveling to Tallahassee and Washington, DC, for work. Eventually I opened up to him on one of our several-hour car trips to Tallahassee about what was happening between Kenny and me. The dysfunction was becoming too difficult to hide.

I explained that I felt like I was on a roller coaster with Kenny and like I was going crazy at times. I told him my friend Lynn had said to look up the term *crazy-making* because that's what was happening. I read the definition to him.

"You need to end it, Marni," Kevin said.

"Don't get me wrong; I love him," I replied.

"What you are describing isn't love," he continued.

I just sat there contemplating his words. Tears were starting to fill my eyes. I knew I wouldn't be able to continue without crying, so I remained quiet.

"I'm worried. Has he gotten physical?" he asked.

"No. It's mostly yelling. He's really intense, but I don't think he would hurt me," I replied.

"Whatever you need, I'm here," Kevin said.

"You're a great friend. Thank you for listening."

He was concerned for my safety but knew there was not much he could do if I wasn't willing to break the cycle.

He instead stayed in the background and continued to be my friend and confidant.

Kirsten Thompson, Kenny's ex-girlfriend and now his enabler, posted to the website She's a Homewrecker that I was involved with Kevin (and others) romantically. The site was dedicated to outing people who were cheating on their significant others. She also sent a letter to Kevin's wife telling her to watch out for me because I was trying to take him from her.

The letter began with, "You would be wise to keep your husband away from Mayor Sawicki. She likes married men and has her eye on your husband."

The last two sentences of the note said, "She is a sociopath and WILL get what she wants. You don't deserve this."

I did not tell anyone when I decided to get married to Kenny. Yes, married. Unless you've ever been in an abusive relationship, this isn't easy to explain. Few would understand.

Abuse is always about power and control. All I can do now is tell my story and own it so that other women might have the courage to leave.

In addition to dealing with my personal relationship with Kenny, I also had to endure professional shame and accusations of corruption, infidelity, and incompetence.

After we got back together following the restraining order, Kenny and I were sitting alone in my condominium. The criticism was becoming unbearable. Out of the blue he said, "If we get married, they can't come between us."

I sat quietly contemplating what he had just said. "How will it help?" I asked.

"If we are married, we would show the world we are stronger together. Let's get married at the justice of the peace."

"When?" I asked.

"Today!" he said.

"But it's already the afternoon," I said, looking up how to get married in Florida.

We agreed we had to go to another county to do it. If we didn't, the news would be out that evening.

We went online and quickly took the online marriage course to get our certificate. With that in hand, we headed to the Hendry County Courthouse.

I told no one.

We arrived just before they closed. As we stood next to the bookshelf in the county clerk's office, we said, "I do."

The clerk asked if we wanted to have our picture taken on the front steps.

"No, thank you," I quickly said.

I had a sinking feeling in my stomach; however, I chalked it up to nerves.

MS. MAYOR

Kirsten, meanwhile, had used Kenny's union email password to access his personal email account. She downloaded emails, text messages, and photos. This information would begin making its way out to the public on social media. She posted how much my jewelry cost, details of intimate emails between Kenny and me, information on my whereabouts that she said "proved" I was dating Kevin Ruane, and quotes from text messages between Kenny and me.

The packet of information she gave to the fire department for its internal investigation was two hundred fifty pages long. She included articles on me, a timeline showing every event I attended while in office, our wedding photos, a picture of Kenny's truck parked in my condominium parking lot, etc. All of it became public record and was included in the final report for everyone to see.

The day after our wedding, we flew to Punta Cana in the Dominican Republic for our honeymoon. Kenny bought the plane tickets, and I put our hotel package on my credit card.

Kenny and me in Punta Cana during our honeymoon.

We both tried to drown out the outside world so we could enjoy our time together, but he kept bringing up old wounds and our arguing started all over again. On our second night there, I asked him why he hadn't called Kirsten, Sam, and Jessica to tell them I hadn't done the things they said I did.

He got upset.

In an act of exasperation, he texted Kirsten.

"Who the fuck are you to put that info out there?" he wrote. "I never gave you the info and that shit wasn't yours to put out. That was my info only needed to defend myself against the injunction, no more no less. I adamantly refused to give that info repeatedly to Jessica. Sorry I ever trusted you. You stole that to be spiteful. You had no right.

"Now, I see who you really are," he wrote.

Kenny became more agitated as the discussion went on. He was also angry that I had called Lynn while we were there to explain why I had gotten married.

Earlier, to show his displeasure, he had left me at lunch and refused to speak to me for most of the day. He had a few drinks after dinner, and when he returned to our hotel room, he let out all his anger from the day.

"Give me your phone so I can see your messages," he demanded.

"No," I said. "I don't ask to see yours, and if you have to ask for my phone, you didn't mean it when you said we were starting new."

"Give...me...your...phone," he repeated as he lunged for it. I pulled it away from him. Kenny, a wrestler during high school, pulled me in and put me in a choke hold. My face was smashed into the bedsheets.

"Get off me!" I yelled.

I reached behind me and used my fingernails to dig into his face and arm. He gripped me tighter. I bit his arm and bloodied the sheets.

"I can't take any more of this!" I yelled.

He let go. With the adrenaline still running through my veins, I shouted, "I just need to end it all!"

I walked over to my bag and took out some medicine to calm my nerves.

"You are not going to harm yourself!" Kenny yelled.

As I opened the lid to the bottle, he came up behind me and tried to take it from my hand. The bottle fell to the floor and the pills spilled. Rather than helping me pick them up, he grabbed his phone and took pictures of the pills strewn all over.

"What are you doing?" I cried.

"Taking pictures to have proof!" he said.

"Proof of what?" I asked.

"That you were trying to kill yourself," he said.

"Kenny, I'm just taking my medicine so I can calm down," I said as I picked up the pills and put them back into the bottle. He went over to the bed and laid down. After collecting the pills, I crawled into bed crying.

We went to sleep.

The next day, he woke up and acted like nothing had happened. The blood all over the bedsheets was a stark reminder of the events of the night before.

Kenny was nice again, so I tried to put the night behind me. We still had two more days left of our honeymoon, and I didn't want to spend them fighting. There was no going back at this point. Once the media found out we were married, they were sure to mock my prior attempt at getting a restraining order only to marry him months later.

Once we returned home, Kenny agreed to go with me to see a therapist. The man came to the condominium to meet with us. On one of his sessions, he asked Kenny to see him individually. He thought Kenny needed to learn how to "self-soothe." That was the last time we saw him. Kenny would never agree that he was more of the issue in our relationship.

It's so difficult to talk about the back-and-forth between Kenny and me. It's even more difficult to physically show what the cycle of abuse truly looks like. I know it looks crazy to the outside world; however, it was constant ups and downs, volleying between meanness and niceness, creating this circle of dysfunction.

We would argue and fight one minute, and then, when he knew he had pushed it too far, he would apologize, buy me gifts, and send me poems, only to repeat the cycle all over again later.

I did the research to understand how abuse is perpetuated in a relationship. Several factors contribute to someone becoming addicted to their abuser. Chemicals in our brains are activated that keep the abuser and victim bonded through effects such as these:

- Oxytocin—bonding, most often discussed in the contexts of motherhood and sex
- Endogenous opioids—pain, pleasure, dependence, and withdrawal
- Corticotropin-releasing factor—stress, withdrawal
- Dopamine—wanting, craving, seeking

These chemicals, combined with the irregularities of the abuse cycle, can create a mindset in which it becomes nearly impossible for the victim to manage their intense emotions and make logical decisions.

There are two psychological states that prevent victims from being able to leave the situation. The first is cognitive dissonance, and the second is called a trauma bond. When in either of these states, the victim's reasoning abilities are completely overridden, preventing him or her from leaving. If a person stays in an abusive relationship for an extended period, this process can happen to the brain automatically.

According to the Shoreline Recovery Center in their article "How Domestic Abuse Affects the Brain" (shorelinerecoverycenter.com), cognitive dissonance reflects the distress and trauma of holding two opposing beliefs simultaneously.

"Individuals often will sit fighting between two opposite reasonings; these can often take [a form like this one]:

1. An abuser is a nasty person who has violated my trust. I have witnessed a pattern of cruelty and evil; [people like this] are toxic individuals I need to get rid of.
2. An abuser is a good [person] deep down; they were having a hard day and didn't intentionally go out of their way to hurt me; it just happened. Their aggression was not indeed at me; [the person] was protecting himself from all the guilt he is carrying for what he did."

When our brains start attempting to make sense of conflicting, opposite information, the process of reasoning and rationalizing commonly begins to happen. This process can begin immediately; for a victim to end the cycle of trauma and get rid of the abuser and the hostile environment that person causes, the victim must start seeing the reality of the situation. They must stop reasoning and rationalizing that the abuse will stop or change!

This all sounds very technical; however, ICADV.org has great information on understanding the cycle of violence. The site shares an image of a circle. In the center is Denial, where the victim tries to minimize the abuse, acts as if it did not happen, or acts as if it will never happen again.

The first step in the cycle is called the Honeymoon. Here the batterer says they are sorry or begs for forgiveness. They promise to go to counseling, or they send flowers or presents and promise they will never do it again. The victim, on the other hand, agrees to stay, attempts to stop legal proceedings, returns, or takes the batterer back, and feels happy or hopeful.

After the Honeymoon stage, the batterer moves into the Tension Building phase. The batterer is moody and nitpicky, withdraws affection, yells, criticizes, threatens, and makes the victim feel crazy. Meanwhile, the victim attempts to calm their partner, nurtures, is silent or talkative, stays away from family and friends, is agreeable, tries to reason, and has the general feeling of walking on eggshells.

The third step is called an Acute Explosion. The batterer will hit, choke, humiliate, rape, beat, use verbal abuse, or destroy property while the victim takes any defensive measures they can. The victim, their child, or a neighbor calls the police and the victim attempts to calm the abuser, fight back, or leave.

After this, the cycle starts all over again, beginning with the Honeymoon phase.

Adding to the story was how Kirsten, Kenny's former girlfriend, reacted to our marriage. She went over the edge.

Kirsten and her group joined forces with Lisa Cohen, Jay LaGace, Lynn Rosko, and members of the Republican Party to publicly shame me as they spread misinformation throughout the community. They pounded social media, television, radio, and print media, and they sent letters to the editor and emails to elected officials saying things like, "The embarrassment for the city just continues to grow. And it's very tiresome to see the same person continually involved with so much of the disruption or distraction."

In one letter to the editor, a commenter said, "You really don't get it! This love/hate relationship between our mayor and the firefighter is just another example of her un-stability!" Another said, "Suggest you Google her name and see every scandal."

The story about me and Kevin Ruane also continued to be part of their narrative. Lisa Cohen posted memes of Kermit the Frog and Miss Piggy having sex with the caption "What two mayors is this?"

Kirsten wrote on a Facebook post in a group forum, "I can't believe no one figured it out long ago. LOL All you had to do was follow her FB page and see all the photos of them together. She has some impressive juggling skills." She posted several messages describing Kenny and my personal emails.

At one point, an anonymous person copied the links to online articles about me into an email and sent it to every mayor in the Florida League of Mayors. I learned of this when I was in Orlando for a board of directors meeting. Mayor William Capote of Palm Bay, Florida, who is a dear friend, approached me asking about the email he had received. I was mortified when he forwarded it.

The email was only a few sentences long. It said, "Check out the Cape Coral mayor's scandals" and included several links to articles about me that came up on Google.

As if having residents coming after me wasn't enough, I was constantly being attacked by my Republican council members (and one Democrat) on the dais.

They would yell "point of order" when I was in the middle of talking in our meetings, disrupting my talking points. The three council members would demand I apologize for my behavior, or they would grandstand against all my initiatives. In addition, they would have residents come to the podium during public comment to call me names or tell me that I needed to resign and that I was crazy.

Council members Rana Erbrick and Richard Leon joined forces and did all they could to discredit me in public. Little did I know what they were planning was much bigger than anything I could have ever imagined.

I now understand what I experienced all those years; however, it would take almost losing my life to make me finally leave him.

CHAPTER 10

IF ALL ELSE FAILS, THROW DIRT

Image is what people think we are. Integrity is what we really are.
—*John C. Maxwell*

During a council meeting in August 2016, my public and private lives were turned upside down by three council members: Jessica Cosden (D), Rana Erbrick (R), and Richard Leon (R), along with a group of residents including Kirsten Thompson and Sam Fisher (R), a member of the governing board for the city-owned charter schools.

They referred to themselves as the Cape Coral Deplorables.

They knew what they were talking about.

That Monday night, there was something in the air, but I couldn't put my finger on what it was. For a few weeks, I could feel heightened tension growing from Leon, Erbrick, and Cosden. I had seen the chatter on social media from residents saying I was corrupt even though there was no evidence to support the charge.

As I rode the elevator up to the council chambers with Jessica Cosden, she was acting nervous and wouldn't look me in the eyes. That same night, Richard Leon was late to our city council meeting. About twenty minutes into the meeting, Richard came up to sit on the dais.

The meeting wasn't going to be a long one, but when we got to individual council member reports, Richard asked the city clerk to put some documents up on the screen for everyone to see. As I watched the back of the room where the reporters sat, I could see them looking through a packet of some sort.

I was confused by what was happening, and then Leon began by telling the council and members viewing from home and in the chambers that I was guilty of illegal activities.

"She didn't properly report gifts received during a relationship and also failed to disclose possible conflicts of interest," he said.

In the fifty-page packet the trio had given to the press were photos taken off social media showing jewelry I had received from Brian Rist, whom I had dated for over a year. There were appraisals of my jewelry and a timeline of all the events I had attended over my years as mayor.

I was in shock because many of the documents could have only come from my house. To have my jewelry appraised, someone in my house had to have access to my records.

I could feel my stomach getting queasy and felt lightheaded. I looked out into the audience, where my husband Kenny was sitting. He looked like a ghost.

Instantly, I knew the only person who could have had access was him.

Our relationship had gotten off to a rocky start, but this was inexcusable. There are no words to describe the betrayal I felt. I couldn't wrap my head around *why* he would give them the documents.

There was something ominous brewing, and I was completely in the dark as to what that was. Was this because I had filed a restraining order against Kenny? Apparently it was.

As I went back through his texts, I couldn't believe how naïve I had been. I saw he had alluded to this circus before I filed my restraining order.

Other council members began asking Richard Leon why he was bringing the subject up in this manner.

"This is not a trial," said Councilman John Carioscia. "Why are you bringing this up at a council meeting? It seems it's more of a matter for the state."

Leon then turned to the city attorney, Dolores Menendez, and asked her to give her opinion on the packet of material he had passed out to everyone but me.

"I agree this is more of a matter for the state," she answered.

I sat silently while Leon agreed he would send his concerns to the state's ethics committee.

I could feel my face flushing. This was another one of their stunts to keep the negative press on me, but it went too far. I couldn't believe what I was watching. I hadn't received a packet, so I didn't have anything tangible in hand to review during or after the meeting.

As the meeting wrapped up, I quickly gathered my belongings and left the council chambers for my car, hoping to beat any members of the press out of the chamber. Standing next to my car was a reporter from the *News-Press* named Frank Bumb.

I found out later that he was part of the group hoping to villainize me. As I approached, he immediately started asking me questions about the packet of information.

"I have not seen the packet, so I am unable to comment," I said, holding back tears.

I got in my car, shut the door, and proceeded to drive off. I cried all the way home.

My cell phone started ringing as soon as I got in my car. It was Kenny, trying to do damage control. I didn't want to talk, so I let it go to voicemail. He continued to send text messages, each with more urgency than the one before.

The media ran the story almost immediately. To block the noise, I had to turn my phone off for the evening.

I took one call from Kevin Ruane. Our conversation was brief because I was trying to keep the tears from falling even harder.

"I'm just checking on you. Are you okay?" he asked.

I could barely eke out a full sentence. "I will call you tomorrow, Kevin. Thank you for checking on me," I said.

I hung up the phone as I pulled into my condominium parking garage. There, I sat in my car and cried in disbelief.

Richard Leon filed his complaint with the Florida Commission on Ethics. The charges were ludicrous. They charged me with taking gifts from then-boyfriend Brian Rist in exchange for votes.

That wasn't all. His complaint charged that because Brian Rist's company was the sponsor of the city's Red, White, and Boom Fourth of July event, he was a vendor for the city. Brian became a sponsor in 2014 because the city was going to have to cancel the event due to lack of funds. Brian, along with a few other local businesses, stepped up to donate the money so the event could take place. He gave the city $40,000. The sponsorship never came before council for a vote, and the city manager did not need the council's input on accepting the money.

Brian also had not approached the city since I had taken office about selling them hurricane shutters. Nevertheless, Leon and his crew claimed that the jewelry Brian bought me for various holidays should have been reported on my campaign finance report because we were not married.

They also said I was a member of the mafia. They claimed I had ties to a man who owned sixty-seven properties near Bimini Basin—the project I was trying to get off the ground.

It turned out that this man, Mr. Cirrincione, had been arrested for bombing a pizza joint in Chicago and had ties to the Chicago mafia. The chief of police and city manager had made me aware of his arrest as soon as we started discussing the project.

I had met him only once for lunch to discuss his goals for his property. The only other time I met with him had been in the city manager's office when he was invited to talk about our plans for the area. Richard Leon and his group claimed that I stayed in this man's villa in Italy when Brian Rist and my family went on vacation for Christmas. Leon and the others said that because I was pushing for the Bimini Basin project so hard, I had to be benefiting from the project.

Finally, Leon charged that I had voted to allow the Dixie Roadhouse to stay open until 4:00 a.m. because I had invested in the place.

My friend Lynn Pippenger had asked to borrow some money for a brief time because she needed to put down a security deposit. I willingly loaned her the money. Kenny knew what the money was for. But after reading the complaint, I could see clearly that Kenny had told Leon and the others that I was an investor in Lynn's bar.

"Cape Coral Mayor's Office under Investigation" read the headline the next day. Cape Coral was the seventeenth safest city in the nation, so ordinarily there wasn't horrible crime to talk about. A scandal with the first woman mayor in the city's history was big news.

Unfortunately, in the court of public opinion, I was guilty until proven innocent.

Most ethics complaints take months before they're cleared up or reviewed. Mine was no different. Leon filed the complaint in October 2016, and the committee didn't review my case and render a verdict until March 2018—a full year and a half later.

My office, meanwhile, was under this big, black cloud.

The Deplorables filed the complaint to either make me resign, dissuade me from running for reelection, or send me to jail.

I didn't learn what was being said during the law enforcement interviews until the case was closed.

Kirsten Thompson, under oath, told the investigator that her group was doing its best to place red herrings in the media to keep the eye on me. Her jealousy toward me fueled the hatred she passed on to Leon, Erbrick, and Cosden.

In the court of public opinion, it was working. While they were talking in the media and posting on social media, telling the entire city I was guilty, I couldn't talk about it.

My attorney, Mark Herron, advised me to not say anything until the hearing. For the rest of my term, my enemies were able to throw anything and everything against the wall to see if it stuck, and I was powerless to defend myself until the hearing.

Imagine going about your day-to-day business talking to friends, attending meetings, working, volunteering, or whatever it is you do on any given day. The people you interact with on a regular basis smile, listen to you, and offer support to your face, but behind the scenes, they're using every little bit of information you share to devise a plan to ruin your career and your life and to put you in jail. They do this with no proof, only hearsay motivated by jealousy, political gain, and sheer vindictiveness.

Imagine how I felt when I finally got to read about everything they did in the findings of the various investigations. I can't express the amount of hurt and betrayal I felt. Most of all, I felt naive and stupid for not knowing it was going on while these individuals looked me in the eye and claimed to be friends.

Throughout this time of turmoil and grandstanding, other women inspired me to keep going. During a very contentious meeting in December after Councilman Leon filed his complaint, my exhaustion was beginning to show. It was during those darkest moments, when I thought I couldn't take much more, that a tiny light would shine through and give me hope.

Inspiration comes in many forms. I received the following note from our city auditor, Margaret Krym, who worked with me on both the audit and budget committees. It came exactly when I needed it most, and I hung it on my bathroom mirror.

> Mayor Sawicki,
>
> During this time when you have been publicly attacked and undermined, I just want to be sure that you know that you are admired and supported by many. You have done an amazing job as the Mayor of Cape Coral. The city has

advanced and shifted its focus from internal bickering to outward vision, growth, and improved accountability. It has been wonderful to watch. So refreshing and inspiring.

I view you as an outstanding leader with so much to offer to the citizens of Cape Coral and beyond. I certainly see your political career expanding beyond Cape Coral. I hope you do not lose heart.

If you must be a target . . . then be a "target out of reach." Find your center and your sense of internal stillness and rest there. Let the whirlwind blow by. You are certainly better than all of it. You can be proud of all you have accomplished and will accomplish.

Please know that you have my full support and admiration.

When you're in the stew, it's hard to see the impact you are making on those around you; but trust me when I say you *do* make an impact. Having the courage to get messy, even when it comes with scars, is how we inspire others. Inspiring others is how we change cultures and companies, and yes, even politics.

My mentor, Michel Doherty, took to social media regarding council member Leon's attack on the dais. He wrote, "Run clean campaigns. You don't need to put others down to make yourself look good. Just a shame. Love this city. I do not want the evil that is now sitting on us reflected on all our citizens who look for the positives."

A few weeks later, someone named Bunny Green, who not surprisingly turned out to be Kirsten, emailed the city clerk's office asking for information under the Freedom of Information Act. She wanted all my emails to certain people working in the city.

At one of the Florida League of Mayors meetings, the city manager was handed an envelope from Bunny Green with my emails inside. It came with a note to him claiming I hadn't disclosed all the documents and emails I had sent and received.

The ironic part is the only way someone would know that was by accessing my actual email. In this case, Kirsten was working for the fire union, Local 2424, with my husband, her ex-boyfriend. He had given her his fire union email and password to migrate documents onto their new union cloud; however, he had the same password for his personal email. She went into his personal account without him knowing and printed out all the emails between him and me.

Many of them had been written before I was elected to office.

Nothing ever came of Bunny Green's FOIA request, but the emails she stole were given to the investigator in an attempt to prove I had broken the Sunshine Law. I had turned in over 4,500 emails to the city clerk for this request. Meanwhile, all these conspiracy ideas were being floated on social media in private group pages. I was becoming infamous.

Four weeks after the August council meeting where Leon released documents accusing me of being corrupt, I filed for divorce from Kenny.

Our entire relationship became too much to bear once I learned he had purposely taken things from my home to give to this group of enemies.

Of course, he had excuses for his actions.

The morning after the council meeting, we discussed the events of the night before. I was still exhausted from crying all night.

"How could you do that to me?" I said in tears.

"Marni, I didn't give them everything in that packet," he said.

His words and facial expressions showed genuine concern.

"You're the only one who would have had access to personal documents like my jewelry appraisals, checks I wrote to Brian for the condominium down payment, and monthly payments, among other things," I said as I cried.

"When we weren't speaking—during the time of the restraining order—I was upset," he said. "I did take the pictures and showed them to Kirsten, Jessica, and Sam, but I didn't give anything to them.

"How did they get them, then? When did you take the pictures?"

"That's what I would like to know," he said. "I promise I didn't give them those documents. I took them when you were away one week and you asked me to stay and watch your dog."

I just sat staring at him with tears running down my face. I was having such a hard time discerning what was true and what wasn't. How could he share my personal information like that if he loved me? What kind of person does this and then wants to get married? Why didn't he tell me prior to our getting married?

It was all starting to make sense. This is what he was referring to before I filed the restraining order. All his ranting was beginning to make some sense to me now. He knew these people were devising a plan to bring me down. He had even *helped* them during the time of our breakup. Who does that to the person they're supposed to love?

He said he was just as furious as I was. To show me he hadn't given any of my information to anyone, he commented under one of Kirsten's posts on Facebook. She had released more information from our personal emails.

He wrote, "I am aware that there's a question about emails from Jay and Kirsten. Let's cut the BS. Real simple. Any emails from my personal, private account not produced by me are stolen from my account being hacked. Individuals and various groups are attempting to use unlawfully obtained personal and private information to defame and damage both Marni and [me] personally and professionally."

Kirsten replied under the post, "Let's explore the concept of stolen. Let's pretend Jack gives Jill a donut. 'Jill, I would really like you to have this donut.' Jill accepts the donut and begins to chew. Before Jill swallows the donut, Jack changes his mind and says he wants his donut back. Jill says, 'Oh no Jack, this donut is too good. I'm not spitting it out.' And she swallows the donut. Did Jill steal the donut from Jack or was it rightfully given to her?"

Kenny replied, "So where did the email come from Jay? Who gave it to you? Never mind, we already know the truth. Thank you for the nursery rhyme, Kirsten, but it wasn't accurate. It would be easier and factual if you just admitted you accessed my Gmail account without permission. You were only ever permitted to access my VP account when we switched carriers. Never were you authorized to go into my personal account. Beyond creepy that you would access my account and share them. So instead of playing cat and mouse games, why don't you just admit you were in my private/personal account without my permission and have shared it with many in an effort to tear both Marni and [me] down?"

I didn't know who to believe. I couldn't imagine he could have written what he did on Facebook if it weren't true. I wanted so badly to believe him. I *needed* to believe him because the alternative was too much to bear.

I knew I didn't have all the pieces to this puzzle of craziness, and I didn't have the time to let it all sink in. The one thing Kenny knew how to do was sow chaos. The more chaotic things were, the more I couldn't see my way out of our relationship.

I tried to leave Kenny in late August. I told him I couldn't get over how betrayed I felt.

"I know you keep going there," he texted me. "That's why you and I need to put it into proper perspective. I know you're bitter with me, but it's not me nor are you fully understanding my commitment to you. You will be able to better process if you understand fully and the big picture. I'm not letting you go through this or anything for that matter alone. I'm here to support and work through this with you, not against you."

He continued, "Instead of looking at the negatives of us, you need to appreciate what we bring together. Are you hurting me? Start loving me, Marni. I'm not throwing away our love. You're angry but it's not all me although you think it is. I'm not the enemy. Giving up on us is not the answer."

"I do love you," I responded, "but when do we love ourselves? I've been writing down my thoughts all day in between meetings."

He wrote, "Do you want to be my wife? You mean more to me than the past and I hope I mean more to you than the past. Nobody has your back more than I do in this life! Don't continue to talk yourself out of us based on a skewed perspective."

"I'm in the soup, Kenny . . . It's me they are gunning for. How can you not see that?" I said.

He wouldn't stop. The conversation continued to go back and forth.

"I see that and I'm the one here to provide support as your husband," he wrote. "I don't think you are appreciating what that really means. You've been distancing yourself and talking with others. Those others aren't the ones that married you and are willing to put everything necessary into supporting you through this. Going this alone isn't going to make it any better. It will be more stress on you. How do you propose you'll be able to do it alone? Am I missing something?"

"I'm overwhelmed," I answered flatly.

"You need to appreciate what my commitment to you really means and brings," he pleaded.

"But most of the time you add to the stress," I said. "I feel as though I can't talk to you because I get so upset and that makes you upset. I have a knot in my stomach coming home most of the time."

He wouldn't stop.

"We got married to last, Marni. The current situation has put us out of whack, and we need to bring us back to center, not make a rash decision while out of whack."

"I'm afraid it's too late . . . no way to reset," I said. "It's just too much to process and get over."

"We both have regrets. I had a lot to process, yet I believed in you and married you. Are you proposing that we are not worth the work?" he said.

"Love isn't enough here. I am angry. I am hurt. I am overwhelmed and I've played it in my head a million times now. There is no way through it," I replied.

He kept going. "So, despite my anger, I believed in our love, but you don't share the same opinion. I believe in us. Apparently, you don't. Have you talked yourself out of us? You need to hear my side."

I sent him a long email explaining why we shouldn't be together. Reading it now, I wonder how I could have ever stayed with someone who treated me the way he did so long.

I wrote, "We can't seem to be able to find the middle ground. I hate bringing anything up that is an issue, because I know where the argument will go. It escalates and we say things that can't be taken back. I still hear you the other night calling me an 'idiot, manipulative, bipolar' and asking who else I've 'spread my legs for.'

"I know you say these things out of anger, but I can't just forget. We seem to say these things, you tell me you're moving out and then come back. I've had that said to me at least 3 times in the last week and a half. We then go back to pretending nothing was wrong, but we never address the problem. Trust is the foundation of every relationship and especially a marriage. When you get upset, you tell me over and over and over its trust that you struggle with. Whenever I read the ethics complaint, I struggle with trust with you. We are just broken."

I continued, "What I'm most afraid of is that we made a mistake by getting married so quickly. I'm afraid of how we undo what we have done. The Kenny I love shows up for a few days and then he's gone. I'm anxious coming home. I'm anxious I may upset you. I'm just plain anxious. And add the ethics complaint stress onto it and it's even worse. Every time I look at the complaint, I can't help but see the vindictiveness in you. It's my stuff taken by you being used against me. How you haven't flipped out at these people still continues to baffle me. I honestly in my heart believe the reason you haven't is because the truth will come out that you said more, or they have more to throw because of things you said or gave them. I'm anxious there is more coming. I can't get past this."

I ended the email with "Punta Cana should have given us both a reason to pause. Not just that night but all the fighting most of the time we were there."

After I hit send, I turned my phone off. Kenny was on duty at the firehouse, so I didn't think I would have to worry about seeing him before I left for the weekend for Fort Lauderdale. I had an insurance trust meeting to attend. Kevin Ruane was waiting for me at Starbucks so I could ride over with him.

Kenny came running in right before I walked out of the condominium. He had fled the firehouse, leaving it without a lieutenant on duty. It took two hours of fighting before I could get out the door.

Mayor Ruane waited.

When I got to Starbucks, I was a complete mess. My face was puffy from crying, and I was so frazzled, he considered driving me to the hospital.

"Let's go," I said. "I need this weekend away to think."

The entire way over to the other coast, we hardly spoke. When I finally turned my phone back on the next day, there were several voicemails and *hundreds* of text messages from Kenny. Reading them all at once, I could see his pattern of going from one extreme to the other: I love you, I hate you. We should be together, you made a big mistake.

That Sunday, Kenny sent me a text that he had sent to Sam Fisher, one of the team of Deplorables. He sent Sam what he had texted Kirsten while we were on our honeymoon and then said to him, "You can pass that on to Kirsten. I should have never trusted any of you. What I did in getting back with Marni was her and my business. Not yours or hers. I never gave that info out and you know damn well after being asked several times by Jessica that I was adamant about not giving it to her."

Then he texted, "I hope you found some peace this past weekend. I love you and I will not give up on us over this crap. I will stand by you through hell if it's the last thing I do. I will not let you fall when you're feeling weak. I'll be strong and fight to keep this ship afloat. I'm not leaving you to go broke and depressed. I love you too much for that. I don't want to fight with you but I'm willing to fight the external negative forces and fight for our love. I'm not giving up as you proposed."

Kenny went on to say he was moving forward with having Kirsten terminated from working with the union due to her breaching confidentiality and putting info out on social media regarding a member (him) and a member's wife (me).

Even though all of that happened, I couldn't be completely done with him. We were still married. Kenny was skilled at turning things around and using my words against me. He knew the right buttons to push. He knew just how to manipulate me.

Once again, I wouldn't leave him.

CHAPTER 11

AN INTERNAL INVESTIGATION

Don't get confused between what people say you are and who you know you are. —Oprah

The following November, the city opened an Internal Affairs investigation into Kenny. When I met with the city attorney, I asked, "Do I need an attorney?"

"No," she responded.

"Then help me understand what is going on here," I replied.

"The investigation is about you," she said, "but has nothing to do with you."

How was I to read between the lines with that response?

The fire department began interviewing council members Cosden, Erbrick, and Leon, along with Kirsten Thompson and Sam Fisher, who was a governing board member at the municipal charter school. They didn't interview me until mid-January 2017.

Kenny, meanwhile, tried to do everything in his power to smooth things over with me. By now, I didn't know who to trust or what had been said behind closed doors about me. It was difficult for me to hear and read what was being said and not be able to respond.

For a year and a half, my name was dragged through the mud, but I was confident the truth would come out once the hearing took place.

I also had to worry about the Internal Affairs investigation. Meanwhile, during all of this turmoil, I continued being mayor. I went to my meetings, read my information packets, went to events, and did my best to hold my head high.

I'm fortunate I had my children behind me. I drew strength from them.

I often wondered why there was so much interest in my personal life. I could understand the professional side. I was an elected official, therefore there were rules to be followed, and I followed them. What I found most ironic was that I knew so many Republican men who were having or had affairs. I had even heard rumors of some elected officials taking bribes for votes, but those rumors were swept under the rug. Looking back now, I could see they just wanted me out of office. I had disrupted their personal and political lives. I wasn't a part of the "old gang," so I was perceived as a loose cannon. I did not have to have any allegiance to them. Plain and simple, I was a threat to them on many levels.

The city investigation continued into the next year. Even though Kenny and I were divorced, it was difficult to just walk away from him. To be honest, I was personally in a tailspin, and I didn't know how to stop it.

Mike Russell and Ryan Lamb, the fire division chiefs, came into my office to conduct the interview for the Internal Affairs investigation. They turned on a tape recorder, and the chief began by asking me if I knew what the investigation was about.

"I do not," I said.

They handed me a few documents. "Do you recognize these?" Ryan asked.

"Yes, they are personal emails between Ken and me," I said.

I was confused as to why they were showing me these emails, which didn't have anything to do with my position as mayor. They were about disagreements we'd had, and some were about strategies we had discussed.

Ryan handed me a few photos and asked if I recognized them.

"These are my wedding photos from Punta Cana. How did you get these?"

Both men sat quiet. And just like that, it dawned on me where this was all stemming from.

Kirsten had gone into Ken's email and stolen everything. I wondered whether she and her people had victimized Kenny as well. I was also beginning to think that Kenny wasn't as evil as I was making him out to be, instead guilty more of being a buffoon and not protecting his, and ultimately my, privacy, in the snake pit. Seriously, though, he had piled so much abuse on me, I don't know if I will ever be able to recognize and sort it all out.

I looked up and said, "These are personal emails between Ken and me. They have nothing to do with me professionally." I paused. "Can I ask you some questions off the record?"

"Yes," said Ryan. They turned off the tape recorder.

"What does this investigation have to do with me?" I asked.

They began to tell me a story of how Kirsten, under the guise of Bunny Green, had sent anonymous emails to the city manager stating I wasn't being truthful about her FOIA request.

The city manager, it turned out, had thought the request odd and called for the investigation.

After investigators Russell and Lamb spoke with council members Cosden, Erbrick, and Leon, they met with Kirsten and Sam Fisher. Each told how Kenny had approached them stating he had information that showed I was corrupt. Kenny was a respected twenty-seven-year Cape Coral firefighter, and they wanted to investigate his allegations.

I was in disbelief about what I was hearing. I was also mad and upset, and felt a bit foolish too. Knowing that everyone had read my personal emails was humiliating enough, but I also learned that Kirsten and the other Deplorables had hired a private investigator who followed me around taking photos. These photos didn't do anything to help their case, but learning they had done that creeped me out and made me just a little more paranoid.

In February 2017, Kenny told me he was retiring from the fire department.

Why was he retiring? I wondered. He had three more years to go to get his pension.

"I'm done with the department BS and just want to be done," he said. He was leaving a hundred grand on the table by retiring early.

In May, the fire department finished its investigation. The findings read like a story from the Real Housewives series.

The fire department concluded that Kenny had "coordinated and engaged in activities with the intent of damaging Mayor Marni Sawicki professionally. Additionally, he hosted meetings at his home with the purpose of gathering and releasing information that would be damaging to Mayor Marni Sawicki professionally and/or politically."

He had also damaged me personally.

The department further found, based on testimony, physical evidence, and acknowledgment, that when "he took the photos of receipts inside of Mayor Marni Sawicki's home, it is our position that Fire Lieutenant Kenneth Retzer coordinated and engaged in activities with the intent of damaging Mayor Marni Sawicki professionally." They found he was preventing me from doing my duties as mayor.

However, Kenny couldn't be fired.

Six months after he retired early, I found he had been tipped off to the findings and retired before he could be held accountable. There was nothing anyone could do to him.

The three council members, Kirsten, and Sam knew exactly what they were doing. They understood Ken and how to manipulate him for their purposes. They were happy to play along and release things to the media to keep me in a negative light for the remainder of my term so Rana Erbrick could run for mayor and Kirsten could get her revenge.

What they hadn't counted on was my resilience. No matter what they said about me, I wouldn't quit. I continued to show up at my meetings and events, holding my head high.

The next crisis had nothing to do with politics. Hurricane Irma was barreling our way in September 2017. The city had to focus on the CAT 5 hurricane that was on course to make a direct hit on our beautiful city.

CHAPTER 12

THE CRITICS CHIME IN

Distracted from distraction by distraction. —*T. S. Eliot*

Social media is how I got my message out throughout the campaign and during my term as mayor. I used it to communicate with my constituents.

My enemies used it as a weapon against me.

The same people who were critics before the election only amplified their voices after it.

After each council meeting when I didn't vote the way the old guard in the community thought I should, that group gained momentum and grew.

One vote at a time, supporters who had once lifted me up turned and joined the group of people who had criticized me from the beginning. As time went on, it became more difficult to keep people who had voted for me and donated to my campaign happy.

I had run on the platform of breathing new life into our city. I had said I would change the city, but actually doing it proved far more difficult. People went along until the changes affected them or interrupted a routine they had been following for years.

Moreover, my professional and personal lives became two parallel paths, dual realities of some sort. What I was doing as mayor was being distorted by the court of public perception. Unfortunately, as they say, perception is reality. And I didn't realize how true that is until it was too late.

Early in my term, a developer wanted to build a car wash on Cape Coral Parkway, our main road right off the bridge coming into the city.

I was against the location he had chosen for the project because first impressions are everything, and I wanted local eateries and shops built along the route into Cape Coral.

According to the city charter, former council members cannot lobby the city for at least two years after they have left office. Marty McClain, who hadn't run for reelection, was working for the developer behind the scenes.

While he never spoke at a council meeting, he did meet with council members individually to push for the project to be approved.

Council member Jim Burch and I would not vote for the car wash at the base of the bridge no matter how much it was pushed.

The car wash developer brought all the employees and their families to the meeting the night we voted. They wore matching T-shirts to show support. Trying to show compassion, I allowed them to stay in our meeting with their shirts on even though our council rules stated there should be nothing within the council chambers to sway a vote one way or another. The owners also launched a social media campaign to garner support.

Their tactics worked.

With a former council member lobbying behind the scenes and others launching a full-scale social media blitz, six of my fellow council members voted for the project. After the vote, longtime city residents who were in the city's political circles took to social media to voice their displeasure with Jim Burch and me for voting against the project.

What surprised me was how quickly some could turn on me based on just one vote. This was true whether the issue was a zoning change or a union negotiation. After this vote, during our council meetings I never again allowed anyone to wear anything controversial, bring a sign, or even clap.

There was never a vote of any significance that was not amplified by both sides on Facebook.

Early on, a few people told me to stay off social media. "Don't go looking for people's comments, because they can mess with your head," they said.

I wish I had listened to them.

At first, I found reading comments a wonderful way to gauge how many in the community felt about particular issues; however, as time passed, social media turned out to be more tunnel vision than anything else. Unhappy people gravitate to one another. Making that easier for some was the fact that they didn't have to say their comments to my face. Keyboard warriors popped up everywhere.

During my first year in office, I was able to stay out of the fray. I used Facebook and Instagram to get out positive messages about our city. I highlighted certain projects and posted whenever something positive was mentioned about Cape Coral.

I started to collect a few repeat haters. Most of them were Republicans, but over time those who were unhappy with either my votes or who I was spending time with in my private life began joining forces.

True, I was naïve about the people in my circle of trust who didn't have my best interest at heart.

I had two kinds of haters. There were Republicans who hated me for what I stood for, and those who grew to dislike me for how I voted or how I was living my personal life as they perceived it.

The first group was the most vocal. The other group was more insidious, preferring to stay in the background while they egged others on to do their dirty work.

The first group was a core of haters who came to our council meetings to stand up during citizens' input and enjoy their three minutes of fame for yelling at us, calling us names, or telling us how we could do our jobs better. This core group would lecture us, telling us that our job was to "serve the people," "work for them," or operate "in the people's house."

My most outspoken critic was realtor Lisa Cohen, a staunch backer of John Sullivan, whom I had defeated as mayor. She was once arrested for bringing a gun to court during her divorce hearing. She was instrumental in filing the recount lawsuit mounted against me.

She also stalked me and posted hateful memes, photos, and comments about me throughout my term.

In my third year as mayor, I stopped into a local bar after a fundraiser for the local Humane Society. Lisa was there. She had just given birth a few months back.

I was sitting with a few other council members when Lisa walked by and began taunting me.

After about the third time, I followed her to the door to request that she leave me alone. She turned around to look at me and said, "Oh, is Miss Piggy trying to defend herself?"

Out of frustration and anger, I replied, "This needs to stop, Lisa."

She just laughed and rolled her eyes. Then I said, "Have you looked in the mirror? There's a new Miss Piggy in town."

Immediately I regretted saying it. This was not who I was. I turned around and walked back to my table. About an hour later, I received a screenshot of her Facebook post.

Her post read, "The Mayor of Cape Coral, just chased me down at Duffy's, got in my face (while slurring her words, because she was so drunk) to call me a 'Fat Bitch.' I reminded her that I just had a baby a few months ago and she kept calling me a 'Fat Bitch' and yelling 'I'm not afraid of you, you fat bitch'..."

She had posted a version of this story in several different Facebook groups. None of it was true, but it was her word against mine.

Following that, I received several hateful messages, comments, and emails from people telling me how despicable I was for saying such hateful things to a new mother.

When I was first elected, Lisa was also the woman who posted about my daughter being "as stupid as her mother." She used her platform to enrage her followers and to push them to harass me. At the beginning of my term, during one of the city council meeting breaks, someone from the police department approached me at the dais.

"Mayor, please do not leave right away after the meeting," he said. "We received a call about someone sitting outside council chambers taking pictures of your vehicle. We have identified the person and are headed to her home to talk with her."

Lisa Cohen was that person. After the meeting ended, the police did a sweep of my car, and they then escorted me to my vehicle.

Lisa posted despicable things about me. "We are formally requesting that the mayor teach a class on the magical vagina," she wrote. "Stay tuned for updates on when that class will be."

Others chimed in. "There has to be something special down there . . ." wrote one woman.

Kirsten Thompson wrote, "I assumed they were all built relatively the same, but you have to wonder . . . Guys, are they all built different? WHAT IS IT?"

The comments continued.

"Only one way to know," said Lisa Cohen. "We must ask the guru LOL."

Finally, Jennifer Smolarz chimed in, "This is nothing special on the outside for sure I just don't get it, maybe she swallows you know we all do that in the beginning lmao."

There were those like Jay LaGace, a Cape Coral realtor, who was constantly stirring the pot with one issue or another. Even though he was a realtor, most of his complaints were about trying to limit who could live in the city, a strange concern for a realtor.

Up until my last year of being mayor, I had never spoken to him personally. I'm not sure where or why he harbored such hatred towards me. People would send me screenshots of his posts, which enraged him.

One night he posted, "To whomever it is in this group sending screenshots of posts to the mayor. I could give two shits. She's a vile person and whatever I post here, I would have no issue saying to her face. Carry on you liberal sheep. I will do everything in my power to make sure she never gets elected to the garbage board here."

And yet no matter how much he puffed out his chest on social media, he would never say it to my face. Ever.

Both Lisa Cohen and Jay LaGace started separate Facebook pages to pass along misinformation to their ever-growing group of followers. Lisa's page was called "Freedom to Oink" because she liked to refer to me as Miss Piggy. Jay started the "Cape Coral Florida Politics the Good, Bad, and Ugly" page. He would not let me become a member. He also kicked out anyone who tried to correct his information.

Jay energized a nasty group of people who heckled and threatened me. This group staged protests outside of city hall and started a mayor recall page on Facebook. They even asked Florida Governor Rick Scott to remove me from office.

When Hillary Clinton didn't win the presidency, one member wrote, "Looks like we have one Democrat down now and one to go in 2017, that share a lot of similarities. LOL."

A year later in 2017, that same man, Dave Stokes, begged Council Member Carioscia to talk to me about supporting him for his city council bid. Carioscia told him to apologize and asked me to support Stokes out of respect for our friendship.

"I won't openly support him, John; but I won't say anything bad either," I told him. Luckily, I never had to serve with him on the council.

Jack Mattachione, a mental health counselor and former council member in Fairborn, Ohio, was another regular who harassed me on social media and at our council meetings.

Mattachione had a rap sheet that included being convicted in federal court of receiving an illegal gratuity in 1999 while in office. During his three minutes at the podium, he would call me names and tell me it was time to step down. On social media, he would call me a communist and a socialist. I offered to meet him for coffee to discuss his concerns, but he never responded.

"I can't sit down with a socialist," he posted online.

Paul Barnes, who was also arrested for domestic violence, was another person berating me frequently at city council meetings. He was more dangerous than many of the others.

When I was first elected, I was sitting in a restaurant with a group of girlfriends after a movie, getting a drink. As I looked up at the menu above the bar, I heard someone yell loudly, "There's the mayor of Cape Coral. You fucking cunt!"

When I turned around, it was Paul.

"Maybe we should go," my friends said.

I agreed. Before I left, I walked up to his date. I leaned over and said, "You should really be careful. He likes to beat the ones he loves."

Then I walked out.

Lynn Rosko, the one they called the Witch of Bergen County, frequently wrote letters to the editor telling readers about all of my perceived incompetence. The last day I was in office, Rosko came to my final meeting and approached the podium.

"No one is going to miss you," she told me in her New Jersey accent.

Typically, she made nasty comments and left the meeting before anyone could address her. That evening I stopped her as she was walking back down the aisle after speaking. I said, "Ms. Rosko, since you always leave before I get to respond to you, let me respond now."

She stopped at the end of the last row of chairs and turned to look at me.

I paused a second, and with a smile I said, "I'm going to miss you too."

The entire audience broke out into laughter. Her only response was to hold up her pinky finger and say, "You don't deserve my middle finger."

With that, she turned and walked out. I later made the 2017 Best Quotes of the Year in the newspaper.

Lynn Rosko was always in the middle of whatever drama was on Facebook. After Richard Leon filed the ethics complaint against me, she posted, "QUESTIONS, QUESTIONS, QUESTIONS: This week was surely breathtaking! Our Mayor stands accused of taking gifts from a married man while not filing Gift Disclosure Forms, amongst other claims of special favors etc."

She parroted Kirsten Thompson and Richard Leon, accusing me and my family of staying in an Italian villa that was supposedly owned by the Chicago mob member who owned multiple properties near the Bimini Basin.

She posted: "Now, questions come to mind; who owned the Italian Villa? Did Brian Rist own it? Was it owned by the developer that wants to develop Bimini Basin as it has been stated that he owns an Italian Villa? Was Brian Rist acting on behalf of this developer? Could this have been a motivation for her to be pushing Bimini Basin?"

She continued, "She is one shrewd chick! In marrying the fire fighter, she finds cover from all sorts of things and she did it in lightning speed! Was it planned is the question????"

Her post was long ... and completely false. That didn't stop Kirsten from chiming in to keep the rumors going. She responded under the original post, "I do know the reconciliation was completely out of the blue and happened very quickly. There had been NO communication since the restraining order. The first communication was late night on Thursday June 23rd while she was in Indiana. She flew home early on Sunday the 26th. They were married on Tuesday the 28th and left on their honeymoon Thursday the 30th. I don't think it was planned but I do think she recognized the benefits and acted quickly to take advantage of them." Kirsten knew at the time she wrote the post exactly what had happened because she had read all of Kenny's emails and texts when she went into his Gmail account without his knowledge.

Lisa Cohen commented, "I thought they were married in the DR."

"She was married on 6/28/2016 in Moore Haven. (I have a copy of it) and then to DR for another ceremony," Lynn replied.

"Sounds like she is Teflon coated just like Hillary," another woman replied.

With every post, Kirsten provided more and more detail about my personal life. Until the internal investigation was released, I had no idea about all of the information she had posted on the internet for all to see.

Another member of the vocal group was Dick Kalfus, who wrote rude and condescending letters about me to the editors of both the *Cape Coral Breeze* and the *News-Press*. The interesting thing about Dick was he eventually changed his mind about me and became one of my biggest supporters. Dick had made coins that had the Ten Commandments engraved on them and sent one to my council office. He had tried with previous councils to get the Ten Commandments hung in Council Chambers. He was voted down, narrowly.

When I received my coin, I called to thank him and promised I would keep it on my desk to bring me luck. He was pleased with that. What I liked most about Mr. Kalfus was his willingness to at least listen.

Despite his snide, nasty letters, I would always respond to him with my viewpoint. Over time, we developed a mutual respect. I could always reach out to him to get the pulse of the group he represented. He bragged that he had a contact database of Cape Coral residents that numbered in the thousands.

At one point, Terri Johns, another member of these hate groups, posted a suggestion that her group meet at the shooting range. She wanted to use my face for target practice.

"I propose a Meet and Greet for the Deplorables that love shooting. As soon as Shoot Center is open let's have some bangety bang bang black powder Range time with one another. Jay LaGace, how about it? Wonder if they sell Marni target sheets!" she posted on Richard Leon's town hall meeting event page.

After residents complained, Leon reported her to the police. The police visited her and advised her to take down her threat.

Terri told everyone that I had called the police on her, and she continued railing against me. She too had a criminal record. She had assaulted a fourteen-year-old girl at a bus stop for saying things to her daughter.

Frequently, it seemed like the Cape Coral Circus.

Mary Orthodox, who was anything but, and her son frequently sought to harass me. Both were staunch Republicans. Mary was a volunteer for the municipally owned charter school. She had been active on my campaign team, knocking on hundreds of doors and leaving my campaign literature.

Once I voted against the gun resolution that was brought to council for a vote, she changed overnight. From then on, she and her son sent hateful emails demanding my resignation. They posted those emails on social media and sent them to the news. Her son went so far as to post videos that looked like they were from the group Anonymous advising me to step down or suffer the consequences.

I understood that simply because I was a Democrat, most of these individuals did not know me personally and were spewing their hate messages. I didn't give them much thought until they joined forces with a group of people who used to be supporters but had come to hate me for various reasons, either because of my voting history or because they were friends with Kenny.

These were the individuals who banded together to create the alternative reality of my existence. They were energized, and besides leaking misinformation on social media, wrote letters to the editor and commented on online news articles anonymously.

Kirsten was the ringleader. It was she who documented my every move and became the most hateful. Kirsten was in love with my husband, and she put in long hours of work to craft a sordid tale of my perceived corruption.

Sam Fisher was an attorney who added his own spin on how I could be corrupt. In the city's internal investigation, Kirsten's group admitted they had worked with Kenny to put red herrings out on social media to disparage me personally and professionally. They were determined and relentless in their attempts to villainize me.

It truly felt like it was good battling evil.

Adamant supporters who defended me also used social media. I am grateful to my assistant Pearl Taylor, Bob Mason, Tabitha Keller, Michel Doherty, John Carioscia, Kelvin Thompkins, Linda Prince, and many others for going out of their way to defend me. Without them, no one would have questioned the validity of the false and malicious claims made by my enemies.

Whenever someone wrote a nasty letter to the editor on the *Cape Coral Breeze* newspaper online, an anonymous supporter would comment under it, "If you believe a public official is guilty of ethics violations and you have evidence to support your claim, then by all means send the information to the ethics commission. Any citizen can do this. Any citizen can do this. It does not take a council person to do this, nor does it take an announcement at a council meeting. You can do so quietly and have the evidence examined by the experts charged to do so. Making an announcement at a council meeting is just theatrics and railroading the mayor in this way is unprofessional and just plain nasty. Whoever counseled Mr. Leon that this was a good idea, gave him some very bad advice. It's not Mr. Leon's role to taint the mayor's reputation in such a public way. He would have earned much more respect had he submitted his claim quietly."

I saved a wonderful post on Facebook to remind me that I was doing something good for my city. Thilo Burkhardt posted a photo of the two of us at my farewell party. His post made me smile.

"Outgoing Mayor of Cape Coral Marni Sawicki and I. In my opinion the best CC Mayor since my immigration in 2008. Thank you for your service, Marni!!!"

Knowing I had people supporting me quietly gave me more strength than anyone could have possibly realized.

CHAPTER 13

PUNCHES TO THE FACE

The world breaks everyone, and afterward, some are strong at the broken places. —Ernest Hemingway

Kenny spent the next few months after we separated asking me to reconsider divorcing. We were divorced in Hendry County on October 11, 2016; however, escaping this destructive relationship wasn't easy.

We attended the divorce hearing together, trying to show our divorce was amicable. We even had breakfast together on our way to the court hearing. After the divorce, I made a solid effort to cut off any communication with Kenny even though I continued to receive text messages from him.

My friends Mayor Ruane and his wife Lynn worried that Kenny would do something to hurt me. I gave Mayor Ruane a key to my condominium in case I didn't respond to my phone.

Two weeks later, on Halloween, Kenny came to my condominium unannounced.

Given there were still two ongoing investigations into my actions, I had become accustomed to staying home alone to avoid being out in crowds. The isolation left me feeling helpless.

I lived at Cape Harbour on the fifteenth floor. It's a beautiful "live, work, play" area of Cape Coral with restaurants, bars, and shops on the first floor and condominiums on top. During the evening of October 31, I took my dog out so he could do his business. I walked out the front door and around the corner, and there was Kenny sitting on the trunk of his car.

He startled me.

"What are you doing here?" I said.

He was drunk.

"Since you won't talk to me, I came to you," he yelled, slurring his words.

"Please lower your voice," I said.

Kenny liked to raise his voice to make a scene, knowing that I was sensitive to people overhearing our arguments.

I offered to call an Uber to take him home even though he lived over an hour away. The ride would have cost me over a hundred dollars.

He continued speaking loudly. I knew it was going to be difficult to get him to leave, but my fear of people hearing him outweighed that concern.

"You can come up to talk, but only if you're sober enough to drive home," I said.

Immediately I texted both Lynn Pippenger and Kevin. I wanted them to know he was there.

It was Halloween night, one of the busiest bar nights of the year, and Lynn texted that she couldn't get away.

I assured them both I was fine.

Once we were in my condominium, Kenny began to tell me again how much he missed me and that I had made a terrible mistake.

The discussion continued for hours.

I didn't have my phone with me to see Kevin's texts asking about my welfare. Around 1:00 a.m., it was evident Kenny couldn't drive home. I told him that he could stay the night but had to leave first thing in the morning.

He agreed and we went to bed.

Not long after I went to bed, I heard the front door of my condominium open and footsteps coming toward the bedroom. Kenny jumped out of bed, and when he opened the door of the bedroom, there was Kevin. He had a key and had come to check on me.

"Why are you here?" Kenny asked belligerently.

Kevin didn't say much but I could see the anger in his eyes. Had I responded to his texts, he wouldn't be in this situation. Without saying much, he turned and left, leaving Kenny to continue to yell and scream at me.

"Why does Kevin Ruane have a key to your condo, Marni?" he yelled.

"He has it in case no one hears from me, or they can't get ahold of me," I said. "I texted him and Lynn when you first showed up to tell them you were here."

"Give me your phone!" he screamed.

"No," I said. "We're not married or together anymore. If you don't leave now, I'm going to call the police!"

He lunged at me and grabbed my phone out of my hand. He picked up his phone and dialed 911 but said nothing to the operator. On the tape you could hear him yelling at me and saying, "Here's your phone!" followed by the sound of him smashing my phone on the tile floor.

He hung up and continued screaming at me as he left.

The 911 operator called Kenny back as he was leaving.

"Yeah, I called nine-one-one," he said. "I'm leaving Mayor Marni Sawicki's house. It doesn't matter. There's no domestic. I'm out of there. Fuck this city!"

He then hung up as the operator continued to attempt to get my address.

Mentally exhausted, I climbed back into bed and covered my head, wishing I could rewind the evening and do everything over.

I hadn't been in bed for ten minutes when there was a knock at my door. Two Cape Coral police officers asked to come in.

Panic sank in.

Once again Kenny had made a spectacle of me, and this time Kevin was involved.

Since I wasn't the one who had called the police, I didn't want to give them any information. Anything I said would have gone into their report, and I knew the media would eventually get ahold of it.

Even though it was early in the morning, I called Chief of Police Dave Newlan to ask if I had to let them in. I knew him well and didn't think twice about calling. He said I didn't have to answer their questions, so I refused.

The next day the media obtained a leaked copy of the police report stating I had called the chief and had refused to cooperate with the officers who came to my door.

The keyboard warriors on social media, including Kirsten and her cohorts, went crazy. Councilman Richard Leon told the news in an interview that I was abusing my power by calling the chief. He even came up with a new hashtag: #Timeforanewmayor.

The entire situation put a huge strain on my friendship with Kevin. We didn't speak again for several months.

Kenny, meanwhile, continued to reach out and try to reconcile. As predictable as the cycle of abuse was, I still couldn't recognize it. I'm not sure if it was the constant noise from social media, the news, or the letters to the editor, but something in me allowed him to come back time and time again. I had lost perspective.

The following April, Kenny and I once again tried to continue our relationship.

My sorority asked me to be the keynote speaker for our seventy-fifth anniversary celebration on Central Michigan University's campus. I flew up at the end of April for the weekend.

Kenny randomly texted me, and this time I responded. We also spoke on the phone, and I explained where I was and when I would be back.

I returned home on a Sunday, flying into Fort Myers. When I exited the plane and came to the non-secured area of the airport, there was Kenny. He had a sign with my name on it surrounded by hearts, and he was holding a dozen roses for me.

"I've been here all morning for each flight that came in from Detroit because I didn't know what flight you were on," he said.

We got back together again.

In June I was scheduled to attend the annual US Conference of Mayors summer meeting. Kenny asked why I had never taken him. I had always taken my children to these summer meetings. They were going again this year. It was in Miami Beach at the Fontainebleau Hotel.

I told Kenny he could come with us.

When we arrived at the conference, Kenny immediately began to get agitated.

"Why didn't you tell me your conferences were all men?" he asked.

"I don't know," I said. "It's government. The people who attend these events are selling things like equipment to the local government. And as I have told you, women elected officials only represent about 11 percent at the local level."

A dear friend who is a consultant at Waste Management came up to me and gave me a hug. We had met during my very first conference back in 2014. He's an older gentleman who has been married for years. We discussed the possibility that I could consult for him after my term ended. We agreed to meet for breakfast to discuss the opportunity more.

Kenny was visibly upset that I had agreed to meet with him. That evening he refused to talk to me.

I woke up the next morning, met my friend for an early breakfast, and then attended the opening meeting welcoming the newly elected mayors into the conference.

When I returned to the room, Kenny was still upset. I told him that if he wanted to attend the next session with me, he would have to change into dress clothes. Kenny liked wearing his fishing shirts and cargo shorts. He wore them everywhere, but I was adamant he couldn't attend without proper dress attire.

He refused.

When I came out of my meeting, Kenny was sitting in a chair right outside the meeting, still dressed in his shorts and fishing shirt. He walked up to me while I was talking to a few other mayors as if to show me who was in control. I immediately left with him.

We began to argue. I told him I would see him later for dinner and left to go back to the conference meetings.

That evening, the conference put on an amazing dinner followed by dancing at LIV in the hotel. I made it a habit to not have more than two drinks at any of my functions while representing my city as mayor. Kenny was never a big drinker either.

I went out to dance with a few friends I knew from Harvard, and they asked me why Kenny looked so angry. I apologized and told them he was fine.

Kenny told me he was stepping outside to have a cigarette. An hour went by, and the night was winding down in the nightclub. I sat outside in the lobby, waiting for him. He had my license and the hotel room key. I couldn't get another key without my license. Finally, he came walking calmly back into the lobby from outside.

"Where have you been?" I asked.

I was irritated. It was late, and I had an early breakfast meeting to attend.

"Out smoking," he replied with a smirk on his face.

We got on the elevator and argued all the way back to the room. My daughter and her friend were still out, but my son and his friend were in the hotel room adjoining ours. Once in the room, Kenny began to argue more vehemently. He was shoving his finger in my face, pointing at me and yelling.

"Get your finger out of my face," I said.

He continued to point and call me names, saying I was a whore and asking how many times I had brought my pimp Brian to a conference.

"Get your finger out of my face and leave me alone," I said.

He kept it up.

I bit his finger.

The situation escalated from zero to sixty in just a few seconds. He paced around the room, yelling obscenities. His finger was bleeding. He pushed me to the floor and threw my shoes at me. Some hit my head, and some hit the wall in front of me.

"Here are your Michael Kors shoes," he yelled. "You took them on all your other trips. With your pimp!"

He continued throwing them at my head yelling, "Whore! Pimp! Whore." With each word, he threw a shoe.

I don't remember pushing the button on my phone to begin recording, but I did. The shoes were hitting me in the back of my head, and I was crying.

"Please stop," I pleaded. "My kids. My kids are next door."

"Well, then you should have thought of that before you went and did what you did!" he said as he lunged at me. He put his hands around my neck and screamed, "You called my kid an asshole once, and your daughter does coke!"

She didn't, but he was concerned only with hurting me now. I kept the phone with me as I got up to sit on the bed.

He wrestled me into a headlock and started beating my head with his fist. My face was buried in the mattress like on our honeymoon, but this time was different. He didn't stop hitting me. He continued yelling, punching, and strangling me.

Finally, he stopped, and I told him that if he didn't leave, I would call the police.

He packed his things and left the room.

My son in the next room heard him yelling and hitting me. He texted his sister to get back to the hotel.

"Yo Ken is yelling a lot at mom. And I think throwing stuff around."

"Go over there," my daughter texted him back.

"ldk I can't go over there. I'm not equipped to deal with this," he wrote back.

"Are they still yelling?" she wanted to know.

"Yes. It's really bad. Ken is crazy."

"Okay, we are coming."

It breaks my heart to read these text messages even now.

I didn't call the police. I cleaned up my face the best I could and laid down on the bed crying. My daughter finally arrived back at the hotel. When she saw me, she immediately wanted me to call the police.

"He won't come back," I told her.

"Yes, he will," she said.

After helping me into bed, she left the adjoining door open—just in case.

A few hours later, there was a knock at the door. It was Kenny.

"Open the door!" he screamed. "Don't make me make a scene!"

I don't remember opening the door, but as soon as I did, I went to shut the adjoining door so my children wouldn't hear him. My daughter jumped out of bed and stuck her foot in the door to keep it from closing.

Kenny went and laid on the other bed with his hands behind his back. While he was gone, he had been texting my daughter back and forth, calling her names.

Madisson told him he'd better leave. He stood up and approached her.

He raised his hand like he was going to strike her, thought better of it, and then returned to the bed.

We both had our concealed weapons in a safe in the room.

"Get my gun and shoot me," he said.

I started walking toward the safe. My children and their friends held me back. Kenny again dialed 911 and hung up after they answered.

"You know the cops are coming, right?" my daughter said. "Just because you didn't say anything doesn't mean they can't locate your phone. You are a firefighter, aren't you?"

When he began to yell again, all four kids started pushing him toward the door.

"I'm not leaving!" he said.

"Then wait out in the hall!" my daughter yelled.

Once he was in the hallway, they shut and locked the door.

The police arrived a few minutes later.

The police asked if I needed to go to the hospital and I said no. I was disoriented and in no condition to be making any decisions.

One of the officers was talking to Kenny in the hall and another one was talking to me.

It was his word against mine until I said to the officer, "Ask my son for his phone. He recorded it."

But he hadn't recorded it. I had.

My son searched the bed and floor until he found my phone. I showed the officer the video.

Immediately, the officer rushed to the hallway to ask Kenny where his gun was.

"I left it in the car," he said.

The police put him on the ground, cuffed him, and took him away. Because I had scratched his face, they took him to the hospital before booking him.

I got a text from Kenny's father, "Where is my son?"

I told him I didn't know.

The police finished getting our statements and taking photos. I finally climbed into bed, still disoriented and exhausted both physically and mentally.

When I awoke, I went to the bathroom and looked in the mirror. One eye was swollen and starting to turn blue. I had finger marks on the side of my swollen neck. He had punched me in the face, so I couldn't smell anything. When I tried to eat, everything tasted like tinfoil, a symptom of being hit in the face.

I called the women I knew at Abuse Counseling and Treatment to find out my options. The police had released him on bail pending his hearing. Who knew where he was now?

I was terrified to go home.

"Be careful driving across Alligator Alley, Marni," the advocate said.

"Why?" I asked.

"Definitely get gas before you get on the road. That first gas station you come to is known for people waiting there for the victim. There have been many murders there," she said.

I was even more on edge. I received a text that the *Miami Herald* had just put the story out online. My phone started going off with calls and text messages. I had planned to cut the trip short and return home, but after seeing the media frenzy that was ensuing at home, I decided to stay.

I thought, Maybe if we stayed on the east coast for a few days, it would all blow over.

It was a nice thought, but not realistic. It was my last conference and I wanted to shield my kids from as much drama as possible.

Unfortunately, the circus was just gearing up.

I called a few of my friends to let them know I was okay. I asked Lynn if she could come and get me since Kenny had driven.

"There's an airport nearby, isn't there? You should be able to get a rental," she said.

Her response made me feel even more alone.

There was a knock at my hotel door. It was Mayor Capote of Palm Bay. He had heard the news about the arrest and had come to check on me.

"I'm so embarrassed, William!" I said to him.

"You have nothing to be embarrassed about," he said. "I'm going to give you an hour to shower and get ready. I'll be back to take you to the conference sessions."

His smile was genuine. We had been good friends since we first met in San Antonio for the Mayors Institute on City Design meeting. He knew me better than most.

On autopilot, I did my best to take a shower. Luckily, my daughter's friend had some heavy foundation, so I was able to cover my black eye and the ligature marks on my neck.

I have no idea how I'm going to show my face at the rest of the conference, I said to myself. I did my best not to think about it.

For the remainder of the conference, Mayor Capote and another friend, Gary Willis, who worked for the Department of Defense, made sure they were with me the entire time. Having their support made it easier to face the rest of the people attending the conference. For three days I couldn't eat much because of the tinfoil taste in my mouth. That week I lost ten pounds.

I made it through the rest of the conference without any additional incidents, though quite a few mayors stopped by to ask me how I was doing.

My getting beat up by my ex-husband was not a secret. The city of Miami Beach placed a few officers with my children for the remainder of the week to make sure they were safe. My daughter got a kick out of having the Secret Service, as she called them, with her everywhere she went.

I found it unfortunate that we needed the extra protection.

On the last day of the conference, we all packed into my daughter's friend's van and headed back to Cape Coral. We almost couldn't fit all our luggage into the van. There were five of us.

Having been duly warned, I did fill up the gas tank immediately after leaving the hotel. As we drove past the first gas station on Alligator Alley, I felt sick to my stomach. I started to shake. Could it be that Kenny was lying in wait for me?

The court had let him out on bail with no GPS monitoring. He could have been anywhere. The stress of not knowing where he was added to the post-traumatic stress I was experiencing. I also knew the media would be waiting for us when we returned.

Chief Newlan called and told me to let him know when I arrived at my condominium. He said he would have officers there to meet me and do a sweep of my parking garage and my unit.

Because Kenny still had the key to my place, I immediately called a locksmith to have him meet me and change the locks.

We turned onto Cape Coral Parkway and approached the bridge. My heart felt like it was beating outside of my chest. I had to fight back my tears. My kids couldn't help but notice that my hands were shaking.

I called the chief to let him know we were about fifteen minutes away. When we pulled into the parking garage, two police cars pulled in behind us. One of the officers told us to stay in the car. I handed him the key to my condominium. Then we waited.

Twenty minutes later, we got the all-clear to park and go up to the condominium. The locksmith came about an hour later.

The next morning, I went to my doctor. He ordered an x-ray, MRI, and CT scan. He noted the swelling around my neck, my black eye, and other bruises in my file.

My assistant was getting a lot of media calls from all over and we didn't know what to say or who to refer them to. I also hadn't heard from anyone from the district attorney's office in Miami.

I called the DA's office and asked to speak to someone handling my case. The district attorney assigned to my case answered.

"My office is getting a lot of media calls regarding my case," I said. "Who can I refer these calls to?"

"I'm sorry," he said. "I haven't looked at your case file yet. Who am I speaking to and why are you getting calls from the media?"

"I'm the mayor of Cape Coral," I said.

There was silence on the other line. "I didn't realize that. I'm sorry," he said.

He then gave me the phone number of his public information officer. I could hear him flipping through my file while we were talking. He gave me the hearing date and time for Kenny to appear.

"Do I have to attend?" I asked.

"No, it's just him, his lawyer, and me who will be there," he said.

"You will most likely have media present," I said.

"In all the cases like this I've prosecuted, I've never had that happen," he said.

I didn't say any more about it. He told me he would call me after the hearing.

The hearing was held the following day. I was home when the local NBC channel started running a promo on my case.

"News at 6:00 p.m.," the reporter said.

My attorney called after the hearing. "I can't believe NBC was there in the hearing. In all my years, I've never seen anything like it," he said.

"Well, it's summer in Florida on the west coast," I said. "There's nothing to talk about, so yeah, I would be news."

The local NBC channel sent a reporter over to Miami every time Kenny had to appear. I was horrified at first, but eventually I began to appreciate that the story was getting the attention it deserved. Hundreds of women reached out to me to tell me their stories of domestic violence.

Because of my status as mayor, I knew I had to prosecute even though every ounce of me wanted it to just go away. With so many people watching, I had to take the case to the end, which meant a trial.

I can fully understand why women drop domestic violence cases. The law in Florida allows the state to prosecute even if the victim refuses to press charges. This seems like a good law at first glance, but most district attorneys won't try a case they don't think they can win, so too often the abuser goes free.

The shame that is placed on the victim is crushing. I felt embarrassed, ashamed, and vulnerable throughout the ordeal. The story was picked up by People.com, Refinery29.com, numerous local newspapers, and Ashley Banfield's HLN show *Crime and Punishment*. Friends shared what they had heard in public. I read comments on social media like, "Well, what did she do to him to deserve it?" or, better yet, "She should resign given she's such a mess."

As if what had happened to me was my fault.

I would snap back, "Instead of concentrating on me in this scenario, how about we just teach people to not put their hands on another person?"

I began seeing a therapist to try to process my feelings regarding the abuse, but my children refused to go. I sent my son articles about why he should see a therapist, and he would send me back links to articles about why parents shouldn't force their children to see a therapist. He was difficult to argue with given his rationale.

"Fine," I told him, "But if you don't go, you can't blame me forever for anything that goes bad in your life!"

He would just laugh and say, "Don't worry. I won't."

I struggled with my own emotions surrounding the domestic violence incident, but I didn't have much time to grieve. In September, Hurricane Irma was billowing toward Cape Coral.

CHAPTER 14

IRMA

The pessimist complains about the wind. The optimist expects it to change. The leader adjusts the sails. —John Maxwell

The Florida Department of Law Enforcement investigation loomed large, but it would have to wait as a potentially catastrophic Category 5 hurricane headed toward Cape Coral. As mayor, I was responsible for the health, safety, and welfare of my community. It was really that simple.

Natural disasters happen, and when they do, residents need strong leaders to see them through. While attending the Seminar for Newly Elected Mayors at Harvard Institute of Politics when I was first elected, I had learned about a course that cities can apply for, the Federal Emergency Management Agency's Integrated Emergency Management Course. It's a grant from FEMA worth approximately $750,000 in training.

Mayor Walter Maddox from Tuscaloosa, Alabama, was brought in to speak to us about his experience with winning the FEMA grant. Over fifty of his city personnel were flown to

FEMA's headquarters in Maryland to participate in a disaster simulation.

Mayor Maddox's city had completed the training about six months prior to the violent EF4 tornado that tore through Tuscaloosa in 2011, killing 74 people and injuring over 1,900. It was one of the costliest tornadoes on record. Mayor Maddox explained how cell towers had been destroyed and that if it hadn't been for the FEMA training, the catastrophe would have been a lot worse.

"The cell towers were hit by the tornado, knocking out our means to communicate. Had we not learned how to work around this, there would have been more casualties," he said.

His city emergency personnel were able to navigate through the obstacles to get people to safety. After he finished speaking, FEMA said the grant application period was still open but would be closing within a few days.

I called our fire chief and asked how quickly he could get a grant proposal together.

"Mayor," he said, "I will make sure we get our application in."

I placed a call to Mayor Maddox once I returned home from the seminar and asked if he could send us a copy of his grant application so we could see what his city had put into the proposal. He had his admin send it immediately. Within two days, the fire chief had submitted our application.

What a wonderful surprise it was to learn we won the grant. Forty cities had applied.

Because of the large size of Cape Coral, FEMA decided to host the simulation in our city. Two hundred people would be involved in the training, including residents and our media.

The disaster FEMA picked for us to work through was a Category 5 hurricane similar to Hurricane Wilma.

To prepare for the training, FEMA came down in June 2015 to look around and determine what resources they needed. The sheriff let us use his helicopter to take the FEMA representative up to see Cape Coral from the air. I accompanied him. Cape Coral has over four hundred miles of canals and is surrounded by water. The magnificent sight that made me fall more in love with my city.

Photo of Cape Coral from the helicopter.

While we were in the air, I asked how other cities had used their training.

"There's an ominous curse that comes to every city that receives our grant," the FEMA representative told me.

"Ominous?" I said.

"Yes," he said, "Every city that has completed this training has had a major catastrophe happen within six months."

"I'm crossing my fingers it doesn't happen to us," I said.

The grant paid for a weeklong training simulation. Every facet of our local government was involved in the training. We spent the first three days learning what our roles were as individual departments.

The last two days were a simulation. They covered everything from how the city manager declares an emergency to how accounting keeps track of resources to the roles of our elected officials.

As mayor, I was the spokesperson for our city. Once a disaster hits, the first thing people want to see is their mayor out in the field and on television. It helps add a sense of normalcy and lets residents know everything is okay. I was so incredibly fortunate to have had this training.

The training took place in August. Cape Coral had not seen an almost direct hit since Hurricane Charley in 2004. That Category 4 hurricane came up the coast and hit Punta Gorda, which is just twenty-six miles from Cape Coral.

Most of our emergency management personnel had never experienced anything like a Category 5 hurricane. To be honest, we hadn't experienced many disasters at all. Because most storms just cause some wind damage, Floridians host hurricane parties during which friends and family get together at someone's home (usually the home with the most protection) to drink and play games until the storm passes. Since moving to Florida in 2011, I had been to quite a few of these.

Everyone who lives in Florida knows a hurricane's path changes by the minute. Models can call for a direct hit one day, and as the storm moves closer and closer, intel gets more accurate. Knowing when to evacuate and how is critical in saving lives. This training gave our city the invaluable gift of preparedness. We came through the simulation prepared for anything.

"We're going to be the first city to break your curse," I told FEMA. "We have nothing to worry about."

It was an empty boast. On January 9, 2016, almost six months to the day since our FEMA training, Cape Coral was hit by the strongest tornado to hit our area in over sixty years. A powerful EF2 tornado stayed on the ground for seven minutes and spanned three and a half miles. Wind speeds surpassed 132 miles per hour. Luckily, there were no deaths; however, the damage was devastating.

So much for beating the curse! Our FEMA training kicked in, and emergency personnel managed the situation like a well-oiled machine.

Governor Rick Scott came down to tour the area with me and Sheriff Mike Scott. We drove through the area hardest hit, and the governor stopped and met with many of the victims.

There was one funny situation. Senator Marco Rubio sent his legislative assistant, Luke, to tour the area with all of us. I had met Luke in Washington when the senator refused to meet with me. After about two hours out in the damaged areas, we returned to our emergency management office. Just as we returned, I received a call on my cell phone from an unknown number. It was Luke.

"Um, mayor, I think you all left without me," he said.

I looked at the fire chief and signaled for him to come over.

"Do you know where you are?" I asked.

"I'm not really sure," Luke replied.

I said to the chief, "Can you please send someone out to where we toured today to pick up Rubio's assistant? We left him out there."

"I'll send someone now," the chief said.

Rubio should have realized how important it was for him to meet with the citizens whom he represents.

The governor declared a state of emergency for Cape Coral so we could have access to low-interest loans for rebuilding. I asked when the loans would be available, but I wasn't getting any clear answers. I needed to be in Tallahassee in the next few days with the Florida League of Mayors. I was asked to sit on the board, and we held our quarterly meeting.

The governor's office called and set up a meeting the next morning. I thought it was to discuss the SBA loans for disaster recovery. These loans were long term, low-interest loans from the US Small Business Administration meant to help disaster survivors return their disaster-damaged homes or businesses to their pre-disaster condition or better. Many in my city would benefit from the loans.

I showed up at his office in Tallahassee and was escorted in. The office was large, and Governor Scott had several items of memorabilia all around. There was a model navy ship, a canned good from a sunken navy ship, and a glass display with his Eagles Scout letter encased. In the front was a large poster with the State of Florida on it that said, Employ Florida.

The governor was a bit awkward as he took me around his office, showing me his favorite items. His assistant came in with a camera and asked if I wanted a photo with him. I politely declined.

Why am I here? I wondered.

I figured it had to do with the loans we needed, so I asked, "Governor, can we talk about the SBA emergency loans?"

"Didn't my FEMA coordinator get with you?" he asked.

"I haven't heard from anyone," I replied.

He handed me his coordinator's business card and told me to call him. As I was leaving, I shook his hand and said, "But you're going to approve the loans, correct?"

I could tell I had caught him off guard.

"Yes, absolutely," he replied.

With that I smiled, turned, and left his office. The SBA loans were approved the following day.

I was getting the hang of lobbying for what we needed as a city. I needed these skills later, in September 2017. Weather alerts were showing a tropical storm forming by the Cape Verde islands and headed toward Saint Maarten and the

British Virgin Islands, gathering strength along the way. The storm quickly turned into a hurricane with the capacity to be a Category 5. We watched it for almost ten days before we knew it was headed our way. Hurricane Irma was predicted to be a direct hit as a Category 4 or 5.

Governor Scott declared a state of emergency on September 4. He immediately started daily conference calls with all the mayors in the state to discuss disaster preparedness and evacuation procedures. If Southwest Florida was going to have to evacuate, we needed to make sure there was gas and shelters in place.

During one conference call, Governor Scott asked if we had anything we needed for our evacuations.

"We need gas, governor," I said. "Most of our gas stations are out."

He asked his FEMA liaison to get on the call. Within a few minutes, he was addressing the situation.

"We will get you gas, mayor," he said.

Tankers were pulling into Cape Coral full of gas the next day.

We hadn't ordered any evacuations yet but knew it would not be long before we had to. The six mayors all met at the county emergency management office in Fort Myers to discuss the specifics with the county manager and commissioners. It was the first of many meetings. Governor Scott and FEMA director Brock Long were present.

To better focus on the impending storm, I sent my children to stay with my girlfriend, Cyndi Bass, in Atlanta. I needed to be at the command center, and they couldn't be there with me. Madisson and Brendon loaded up her car with our cat, dog, and pet snake and headed north. It took a full twenty-four hours for them to get there due to the heavy traffic of people evacuating. They weren't happy about leaving, but they knew I needed to be sure they were safe.

All the mayors met again right before the storm hit. I had already spoken to the county manager and knew we would be declaring evacuation of two-thirds of my city at 2:00 p.m.

Almost 135,000 people were in the first wave of evacuations.

I was the only woman in the meeting and the only one who didn't have a chair to sit in. Nor was I offered one. I had never really felt like the stepchild of the county until that day. As the men sat around the table discussing their own areas' evacuations, Mayor Ruane started talking about saving the vegetation on Sanibel. He was also concerned because his residents expected concierge service, he said. He wondered if he would be able to get them to get on the buses to be evacuated. I wasn't sure what he was expecting the county to do about it.

Mayor Ruane was also upset because he had initially been told that he and his family could shelter at the Lee County Command Center. When that decision changed, he was left to find a hotel for all his family. He was not happy. He was used to getting his way.

I was on edge knowing the task before me, and I was getting frustrated listening to talk about vegetation when so many people in my city were about to be uprooted.

Only the county manager and I knew we were getting ready to evacuate Cape Coral. I asked him, "Mr. County Manager, are we all set for the announcement at 2:00 p.m.?" We were only ten minutes away, so I needed to make sure we were all set with the emergency broadcast.

"Yes, mayor," he replied. "We are good to go."

"Well," I said, "I'll be waiting in the other room where we are holding the press conference."

I left the room, but I could feel all eyes on me as I walked out. The mood abruptly changed. I went and stood by the podium. It was a very solemn time. Weather experts were calling for parts of southwestern Florida to see storm surge inundation of ten to fifteen feet above normal tide levels.

If people didn't take this seriously, we could have devastating losses and people could die.

Brock Long of FEMA kicked off the press conference. Jimmy Patronis, the new CFO of Florida, was also present. They then handed the microphone over to me. We had divided my city into areas A, B, and C. Areas A and B were at the most risk for storm surge and flooding.

I stepped up to the podium and said as calmly as I could, "Effective immediately, Cape Coral is under a mandatory evacuation for Areas A and B."

A map of the areas was on the board next to me. I gave out instructions for curfews and explained how emergency calls would be managed once the storm winds picked up. I was surprisingly calm.

Because our entire city was below sea level, only a few shelters were available in the northeast area of the city. We were still struggling with whether or not we should allow pets. Lee County had one pet-friendly shelter, but we knew that wouldn't be enough. If the hurricane was a direct hit, we could be without food or power for days. There was nothing we could do but open all shelters to pets.

Our goal was not to get people into shelters but to get them to leave the area; however, hundreds of people had nowhere to go but a shelter. We opened the school farthest from the bay for one shelter. We knew it wouldn't be enough, but there were few options.

I was staying at a girlfriend's home. She took her daughter and left, leaving me to figure out how to put up the hurricane shutters. I asked on social media if anyone had extra wood and time to help me get shutters up. Before I made it home that evening, people had already come together and boarded up her house.

My community was amazing like that.

As Hurricane Irma barreled toward us, the mood in emergency management quickly changed. We desperately needed people to heed the call and evacuate, but many refused to leave, having experienced too many evacuations after which storms either were downgraded or changed direction.

The worst part of my job was telling people that when winds reached 45 miles per hour, we would no longer be able to send emergency personnel to help them. We just couldn't risk the safety of our staff. In addition, our bridges would be closed. If they stayed, they needed to understand they would be on their own until the storm passed.

I was giving constant updates on social media, and as the winds started to pick up, I also went on national television on multiple stations to keep everyone up to date on what was happening. I talked with Brian Williams from NBC, the Weather Channel, our local stations, radio stations, and even a Canadian TV station due to the state's many snowbirds who have permanent homes in Canada.

Mayor Sawicki interviews with the Weather Channel.

Just as winds were reaching the 45-mile-per-hour threshold, my friend Lynn texted me.

"Hey," she said. "We decided not to evacuate. We have seventeen adults, eleven kids, and eight dogs and cats at the bar to wait it out."

I felt sick to my stomach and more worried than I have in my lifetime. Her bar was expected to be ground zero for the storm surge, now predicted to reach thirty feet, which meant it could very well engulf her bar and sweep away everyone inside. I wondered how many other residents had decided to do the same thing, and it terrified me; however, I had to be strong. People were depending on me to show strength before, during, and after the storm.

Needing to calm my nerves, I stepped into a small office at the command center, where all emergency personnel were sheltering and monitoring the storm, to do a short meditation. Meditating has always brought me calm and helped me gather perspective. I needed to make sure I held myself together.

As I sat there on the floor meditating, at least two people walked in on me. They closed the door as quickly as they opened it. When I was finished, I walked out feeling a sense of renewal and calmness. I headed to one of the offices again to do another interview about how the storm was progressing and what we were seeing on the ground.

"So, you meditate, huh?" said a firefighter.

"What?" I replied.

"You were meditating in the other room," he said.

I replied, "And?"

He just laughed. Multiple people approached me to say the same thing. I found it odd that so many paid such close attention to what I was doing.

I got back to doing my interviews and meeting with the public information officers to make sure I was giving out the most accurate information. I had been talking to an NBC producer who had worked on Lester Holt's news segment and was in Fort Myers for the storm. His name was Alan Cohen. He was a great sport, and he kept my spirits as light as possible whenever we spoke. At one point, he asked me if Lester could broadcast from Cape Coral after the storm passed.

"If you can find some area with lots of destruction, he can stand in front of that, and it would be great," Alan said.

"I'm not letting you come in and scare my residents to death if the damage is not as bad as expected. Go to Naples and scare those people," I replied.

He laughed hard. We stayed in touch for many years after the storm passed.

The eye of the storm finally reached us, and the sun started shining. Everything was calm. We knew, though, that this was only temporary.

Once the eye moved across, we still had the back end of the storm to contend with. A crew from the fire department was getting ready to go out and assess damages before the winds started back up.

I wanted to go to see for myself, but the fire chief didn't want me to go.

"Have I ever asked for permission before, chief?" I asked.

"That would be a no, mayor," he said with a laugh.

I grabbed my bright yellow raincoat and headed to the fire truck. What struck me most was how dark it was around the city. There was not a light in sight, especially in the north. Power lines were down, and there was flooding in multiple areas; however, all in all, besides a few large, downed trees, we had fared well. At least for this first half of the storm.

The roads were covered with water, and it was difficult to see where they began and ended. As we drove, I could see that the canals were virtually empty. The water had disappeared, and we could see the bottom of the canals. I had heard about this happening during storms. The intense winds were persistent from the northeast. Water had been pulled away from the coast.

The retreating water led to tide levels more than three feet lower than normal. The problem is how the water returns. Storm surge, again, was foremost on my mind.

When the center of the storm moved north, the winds reversed direction, coming from the west or southwest, which sent water levels surging back to the coast. We returned to the command center just as the winds began to pick back up. We were in for another round. I prayed everything would be fine.

The second-half winds were brutal, reaching 140 miles per hour. There wasn't anything to do until the storm passed. We were getting 911 calls from residents. They would have to sit tight until the winds dwindled to under 45 miles per hour. The wait was excruciating.

I had faith that we would all be okay. The storm surge we feared never materialized. The storm slowed as it approached Naples, and water from our canals was dumped on that city, which caused terrible flooding. The storm changed the landscape of our area, and we knew it would take time to repair all the damage.

After the storm, the deputy fire chief made a joke about me meditating.

"You should be thanking me," I said, laughing.

"What for?" he asked.

After being up for three days straight, I felt a bit slap-happy. People had been poking fun at me for meditating, so I figured I would play it out.

"Because I single-handedly saved Cape Coral," I said.

He chuckled. "And how is that?"

"Because I put everyone in my infinite light of protection," I said.

He looked at me to see if I was serious. I was grinning. We both laughed.

I was getting text messages from friends all over the United States saying they had seen me on television. The entire experience was surreal.

Hurricane Irma was the costliest hurricane in the history of Florida. It caused over $50 billion in damages, surpassing Hurricane Andrew. Over 65,000 structures were damaged in Southwest Florida alone.

After the storm, the six mayors met with the county manager again. President Donald Trump was coming to our area to survey the damage. The Republican mayors were talking about going to see him.

Peter Simmons of Bonita Springs said with a laugh, "If you want, mayor, I can see if I can get you in to see him."

"If I need to be invited to discuss the massive damage done to my city with my president, then there is a problem," I said. "Fuck Trump."

The room got quiet.

Trump visited Naples. He and Melania, who wore her high heels, passed out hoagies as they surveyed the damage.

Hoagies. For one of the richest cities in America. There were several surrounding cities that needed food and water assistance. For Trump, that didn't matter.

I never did meet with him. The cleanup just to get to some sort of normalcy took weeks. We were more fortunate than other neighboring cities. Yes, we had damage, but it wasn't as bad as it could have been. The whole community came together to help each other through the crisis. From removing hurricane protection from houses to passing out food and water, the citizens of Cape Coral were there for each other. I was so proud of the city I represented.

With the disaster over and cleanup efforts on the way, it was time for me to focus on the impending FDLE investigation. The year and a half of scrutiny was tiresome. My term as mayor would be over in November, and it was time to clear my name.

CHAPTER 15

THE FDLE INVESTIGATION

Difficult and meaningful will always bring more satisfaction than easy and meaningless. —Maxime Lagacé

I have always considered myself an open book. I believe in being as transparent and authentic as possible. As I have aged, I have become more comfortable showing my authenticity. Running for mayor, my beliefs were constantly being questioned or, worse yet, contorted into something not remotely true.

After I announced my candidacy, one of my first speaking opportunities was at BUPAC, which stands for Businesspeople United Political Action Committee.

BUPAC has always been predominantly Republican. Membership consists of people from across the county. Given I had lived in Cape Coral for only a few years, I was not well known and therefore took many by surprise when I announced I was running for mayor.

On the day I spoke, my opponent, Vince Cummings, made sure the room was packed with his supporters. I was nervous but determined not to let the packed room intimidate me. To sum up my overall performance, I was terrible. I let Cummings' group take over my platform as they shouted questions at me and then refused to let me answer.

"Where do you stand on abortion?" one man shouted.

"What about the Affordable Healthcare Act?" chimed in another.

My response was the same: "Tell me how I can effect change in those areas as mayor, and I will answer. My duty is to focus on the health, safety, and welfare of our community."

I had said this prior to becoming mayor. Local elected officials never take a role in setting policy at the state and federal levels. And Cape Coral had never reached out beyond its own city limits.

The final question was from a former Cape Coral council member, Pete Brandt. He had been part of Mayor John Sullivan's "Fab 5" when he was on council.

"Who did you vote for in the last election?" he asked.

"I'm pretty sure that's none of your business," I said.

I could see Vince Cummings taking pleasure in the carnage; however, he gave me a gift as I made myself a promise never again to be caught off guard like I was in this meeting. I would spend almost every waking moment learning everything I could about the past issues that plagued our city.

All my life, I've had women who supported me and women who did not. But a small subsection of the non-supporters took it to the next level. It's one thing not to agree with someone, but when a person goes out of their way to harm someone, physically or psychologically, something is wrong.

Voting someone out of office is far different from trying to ruin their career or, worse yet, to ruin them as a person, and yet that is exactly what happened when Kirsten Thompson and her group of friends filed a complaint with the Florida Department of Law Enforcement (FDLE). The complaint once again charged that I had wrongly accepted gifts from Brian Rist and failed to disclose conflicts of interest, including a charge that I had allowed the Dixie Roadhouse to remain open longer at night when I was a secret owner of the bar. The charges were ridiculous, but I was powerless to do anything about them. The hidden goal was to disgrace me in the media, and in that they were doing an excellent job.

Kirsten filed her complaint after she, Richard Leon, and their little group decided their previous efforts to ruin my reputation were taking too long. They pressured the city manager's office to act, so an Internal Affairs investigation was sent to the FDLE.

The irony was that Kirsten and her group had helped get me elected. They had coached me, defended me, and showed up at debates to support me.

I won every single straw poll cast in every debate. Kirsten would advise me on questions and give me the background on what had happened in the past. How she could support me while also dating Kenny is beyond me. She knew I was dating him. The only explanation was that Ken had played us both. In fact, he had most of the community fooled. Being that he was a twenty-seven-year lieutenant in the fire department, vice president of his union, and a board member of the political action committee, his reach was far and wide.

People trusted him. Most believed he was the epitome of integrity. He certainly portrayed himself that way.

At first, I was angry that the city had launched an internal investigation into Kenny's activities, but I came to appreciate and be grateful they did. Without this investigation, I would never have known exactly what fueled these investigations.

Their testimonies were released complete with their words, verbatim. Having that insight brought everything full circle. Just because they were supporting me did not mean they weren't watching and taking note of everything I was doing. Kirsten submitted a timeline for everything I did throughout my time in office. Again, they painted a picture and cropped me in.

The fact that I was an open book only served to help their cause. Kirsten and her group—Sam Fisher, Jessica Cosden, and Richard Leon—kept track of people's comments and tried to piece them together to make their case.

When I received a call from Special Agent John King of the FDLE, I asked my attorney what I should do.

"Should I go ahead and meet with him?" I asked.

"You're not obligated to, but it's up to you," he replied.

I already knew Brian Rist was not going to meet with him. The burden of proof was on them.

Meanwhile, my kids nominated me for the *News-Press*'s Politician of the Year award. They wrote a touching letter about all that I had accomplished as mayor. It was significant. Brian Rist had been nominated for Business of the Year.

I received a call from the editor of the paper regarding my nomination.

"Unfortunately, with the investigations still ongoing, we have decided we can't allow you to be considered for the award," Tom Hayden said.

"But Brian Rist is still going to be considered?" I asked.

"Yes," he said.

"You do realize that if I am guilty of anything being said about me, Brian would be guilty as well, right?" I said.

"He isn't under investigation," he said.

The Internal Affairs investigation had already concluded with no findings of guilt. The findings were released but were mostly ignored by the media. Controversy makes good news.

In the summer of 2017, Kirsten, angry that the other investigations were taking too long, insisted that the city manager send the complaint to the FDLE for review.

An investigation was opened, and Special Agent King was assigned to my case. Kirsten's testimony during the internal investigation was enlightening. In it she gave the entire history of her love affair with Kenny. She said she became jealous when I was "making googly-eyes at him when he was sitting next to me."

When she began working with Ken at the fire department, she said, he kept his distance from her.

"I was hearing rumors he was dating Marni Sawicki."

When she learned it was true, she said, she still "loved him dearly and could not move on." In March 2016, she said, he began calling her. This is when he told her I was an investor in the Dixie Roadhouse. He said I was freaking out because as an investor I could be in trouble for voting to extend the hours of the restaurant.

He then said he needed to talk to her, she said. He had ended his relationship with me and he hadn't stopped thinking about her. He said he loved her. She then drove by my house and noticed his truck.

During the Internal Affairs investigation, Jessica Cosden testified that it was Kenny who provided the information that he stole from my phone, not to prove I was corrupt but to hurt me. She said he never provided any proof that I had invested in the Dixie Roadhouse or that I had done anything wrong.

When I finally met with Special Agent King, it was October. Hurricane Irma had pushed the investigation back two months. My attorney, Mark Herron, was present during the questioning. I was asked about everything written in the Ethics Commission complaint as well as in the Internal Affairs report.

I could not read the agent well enough to tell whether he believed me or not. I had to wait for the findings.

I had announced in March that I was not going to seek an additional term. My children and I needed time to heal. The decision not to run was a difficult one. I loved being mayor. The feeling of being able to initiate large-scale change was gratifying. I wrote an op-ed explaining my position.

The reason I had run, I wrote in my op-ed, was because I knew I could make a difference. I had run to increase transparency and accountability in the city government, strengthen our local economy, and improve our community's quality of life.

I wrote about how I had listened to our community, holding town hall meetings throughout my term and speaking often through the years. I wrote about how I had added transparency to our budgeting, how Cape Coral had been selected by Bloomberg Philanthropies, and how I had revamped the city website and the level of service citizens received from all departments.

We had reduced regulations for businesses and grown our commercial base. We had improved the quality of life in Cape Coral in so many ways.

We continued to support the revitalization of South Cape Coral. We approved a $6.5 million game-changing streetscape project for Forty-Seventh Terrace, selected a project manager for Bimini Basin, improved medians throughout the city, and put in sidewalks, bike lanes, and streetlights.

We had also completed a Parks Master Plan and equipped our first responders with much-needed vehicles, equipment, and body cameras. We had addressed pay parity and raises for city employees that had not been addressed in seven years, all the while remaining fiscally responsible with every decision.

Fighting for improved water quality had been a priority from the beginning, which had inspired Cape Coral to join 164 municipalities and 19 counties affected by damaging water pollution and sign on to the largest regional compact ever initiated in the nation.

"I am proud of our city's accomplishments," I wrote. "However, with both of my children now attending college and the number of hours required as mayor, I am choosing to focus my energies on building my company when my term ends. Therefore, I am making the difficult decision not to seek reelection. I am announcing this early in hopes that those in our community who have a desire to move our city forward will consider running.

"Now is not the time for complacency. Strong and caring leaders won't get elected unless we all take the time to get educated on the issues and most importantly, VOTE—to allow the cape to continue its forward momentum. I believe it's critical we elect forward-thinking people who will continue to improve our city and grow it to its full potential."

I admonished my successor to take active roles in the Florida League of Cities, League of Mayors, US Conference of

Mayors, and other organizations to bring back great ideas to improve our community.

"As one of the largest 150 cities nationally," I wrote, "Cape Coral needs to be constantly thinking outside the box to find more efficient ways of doing things. Our residents and officials must continue to fight for our local Home Rule authority and water quality by communicating our specific needs to our state representatives."

I concluded, "For the remainder of my time in office, I will continue to ask the tough questions. I will do the right thing for our city, regardless of political opinions or the loudest voice. I want to ensure the best policies, practices, procedures, and controls are implemented for the betterment of our city and our residents. Thank you for giving me the opportunity to serve you. It has been an honor."

My haters took to social media to rejoice.

It was the right decision, however.

When he read the op-ed, Councilman Jim Burch called me.

"Mayor, can I convince you to run?" he said.

"Jim, I need a break. It is time I focus on myself," I said.

"I don't think I want to sit up there on the dais without you," he said.

Jim had become a wonderful mentor and friend. He had been appointed mayor before Sullivan was elected, when Mayor Eric Feichthaler resigned to run for county commissioner. The two of us had gotten off to a rocky start. He had aligned himself with one of my opponents, A. J. Boyd, during the primary election, but when I won, the unions had backed us both. He served on the board of the League of Cities and proved that he would work diligently to improve the quality of life in Cape Coral.

While we debated many issues and didn't always see eye to eye, I had come to respect him and his wealth of knowledge.

Jim announced his candidacy for the upcoming election. Eleven days later, he dropped out of the race. He called me the day before.

"I can't do it," he said. "I don't like the direction this election is going."

I agreed. In the *Breeze*, Jim derided the political scene in the city, the state, and the nation.

"Abysmal," he called it.

Councilmember Burch was a wonderful elected official. Repeatedly, he proved he was serving for the right reasons. In the current political climate, I'm afraid too few people are willing to jump into the ring now.

Yes, elections do have consequences.

CHAPTER 16

BREAKING FREE

New beginnings are often disguised as painful endings.
—Lao Tzu

The FDLE and Ethics Commission investigations did not wrap up until I was out of office. The trial for my ex-husband Kenny began in January after I left office as well.

After the new Cape Coral mayor, Joe Coviello, was elected, everything changed. I had supported Joe. In fact, Kenny and I were the reason he ran in the first place. For years he had been the chairperson of the Budget Review Committee.

As a voting member of the committee, I came to appreciate how he ran his meetings. He was engaged and open to new ideas but not short-sighted.

When I decided not to run for reelection in March 2017, Kenny and I met Joe and his wife Diane at Cape Harbour for dinner to discuss his candidacy. It took some convincing that he could win, as he was not overly confident. I agreed to give him my 2013 playbook along with campaign material to help him craft his message.

For the first few months, he relied heavily on my knowledge; however, as Republicans began to pressure him and he won the union endorsements, he asked me not to attend his events anymore. He also returned my campaign donation, stating he didn't think it would help him on his finance report.

When he ran for mayor, he was no longer the man I had come to know on the Budget Review Committee. That he pandered to his Republican base in a nonpartisan election saddened me.

I respected his wishes and didn't attend any additional events. After everything I had done to help him get through the primary, it was hard for me to accept the way he and his wife treated me. Still, after he won, I stopped by his election party to congratulate him and wish him good luck.

I wasn't there long, but that didn't prevent someone from taking a photo of me giving him a congratulatory hug and posting it all over social media.

All five of the city council candidates I endorsed were elected in November 2017 even though members of the community pushed hard to defeat anyone connected to me. The outcome said more about my term than anything else. The overwhelming majority of residents had been happy with my term as mayor.

Dick Kalfus, the Republican who had opposed my candidacy in the beginning, penned a letter to the editor saying, "As for the Mayor, we see her as a passionate executive, doing her job and working for the citizens." He continued, "The Council needs to salute this Mayor for demonstrating how important it is to value the tax-payers dollars and doing it on no uncertain terms."

Even now, I get messages periodically on social media letting me know much I am missed.

Members of my team held a farewell party for me at a local restaurant after the swearing in of the new council members. While many people attended, the very people I had helped get into office did not show. It was a stark reminder of how quickly elected officials are forgotten once they leave office.

After the party ended and I was driving home, I felt an overwhelming sense of relief. I also felt like I was about to have a panic attack.

Leaving office was bittersweet for me. I loved serving my community. I loved the positive changes and the progress that the city made under my tenure.

At the same time, there was this terrible feeling of loss I cannot quite explain.

I needed to get away for a while. When I got home, I quickly packed a bag, grabbed my dog Brady, and headed to a hotel on Fort Myers Beach. I spent the week decompressing. Only my children knew where I was. My daughter came to stay with me a few times, but mostly I laid in the sun and tried my best to let go of the anger, grief, and sadness in my heart.

It unfortunately took years to overcome.

The new council's first order of business was a vote to reimburse my attorney's fees for the ethics complaint. It was a small victory, but a victory nonetheless.

I flew to Michigan for a month at Christmastime to put together case documents for the trial of my ex-husband, which was scheduled for February 2018. Having to print out old text messages and voicemails from Kenny was difficult. Given I had been in office when the assault happened, I'd never had time to really process the events that took place that night in Miami. Reviewing the internal investigation report along with testimony from Kirsten and her group only helped to fuel my anger and disbelief.

I put together two large four-inch binders of information to send to my attorney. Kenny's attorney then scheduled depositions for my children in January. On our way over to Miami, I told my kids, "When you go in to meet with Kenny's attorney, do not be nervous. Just tell the truth."

It was the only discussion we had regarding the depositions. We arrived in time for the district attorney to briefly explain how the day would go. As we walked up, he had a box under his arm.

"You have officially gone from a binder to a box!" he laughed.

He was trying to keep it lighthearted; however, I was having a hard time with the prospect of going to trial.

My son went first. Kenny's attorney called Brendon into the room to begin an hour-long deposition. The longer my daughter sat in the hallway waiting for her turn, the angrier I could see her get. She was the one who had confronted Kenny that night in the hotel room.

My children and I suffered from post-traumatic stress disorder; however, it didn't become clear just how bad it was until we were forced to recount the events of that evening. They questioned Brendon about whether we had discussed the events as a family and whether I had told him what to say to the authorities.

Madisson went in directly after Brendon. When I walked by the door on my way to get something to drink, I could see her sitting with her back to the door, her right leg crossed, and her left arm draped over the back of the chair. I knew his attorneys were in for a surprise.

She may only be five foot one and 110 pounds, but her personality filled that room. Her deposition seemed to take forever. When she finally came out of the room, you could tell by her walk that she was still riled up.

"They asked me if Brendon and I had discussed the night of the assault with you, Mom. When I told them no, they asked me again, just with a different question," she said.

"What did you say?" I asked.

"I told them, 'If you're asking me if I continuously asked my mother about the worst night of her life, forcing her to relive it over and over, the answer is hell, no!'" she replied.

The district attorney went in to talk to Kenny's attorney after both kids were finished. Their meeting did not take long.

When he came out, he said, "They would like to speak with you, Marni."

I agreed to go in.

When I entered the room, I sat in the chair to the right. My attorney sat on my left. There was a six-foot table separating the two sides.

Kenny's attorney began, "I'm not sure if you know much about me, but I lived in the Fort Myers area for quite a few years. I used to be the assistant district attorney here in Miami as well."

Feeling irritated, I asked, "Why do I care about your background? I don't need to know you. You are the guy representing the guy who beat me. All I need to worry about is that this guy"—I pointed to the district attorney next to me—"can kick your ass in court."

"Can you kick his ass?" I asked my attorney.

"Yes, I believe I can," he replied.

Staring directly at the other attorney, I said, "There. Now that is all I need to know."

Kenny's attorney was becoming visibly uncomfortable. "Look," he said, "Let me just come out and ask you. What is it you want here?"

"For Ken to be held accountable," I said.

"So, a trial?" he said.

"Yes," I replied.

"You realize I can take that trial from you, and there will be no jury, right?" he continued as if he was going to scare me into submission.

"If I'm not mistaken, a judge still has to hear my case, doesn't he?" I said as I looked over at my attorney.

"Yes, but if my client takes a plea, there isn't anything you can do about it," he said.

"You know what? I think I'll take my chances," I said.

As the meeting wrapped up, I stood up to leave and turned to face his attorney again. "When will you be scheduling the depositions for my children's friends who were with us in Miami and witnessed everything?" I asked.

"What witnesses? There was not any mention of additional witnesses in the police report," he said, looking shocked.

"I don't care what the police report says. There were two more witnesses present," I said.

At this point, the district attorney chimed in to say that yes, there were two additional witnesses.

"We'll get back to you," Kenny's attorney said, looking even more agitated.

With that, the meeting was over, and we walked out. After the door shut, my attorney looked at me and said, "I now know you're a badass, and your daughter has ice water running through her veins!"

I smiled. "We've been through a lot," I replied.

I had told the kids that I didn't want them to have memories of these trips to Miami for the depositions and trial. We were spending the remainder of the day in downtown

Miami. Our first stop was sushi for lunch. We then drove over to see the Wynwood Walls. Wynwood was established in 2009 by the legendary Tony Goldman. The neighborhood's buildings have extraordinary art murals on them. Walking around in this outdoor museum did much to brighten our spirits.

Wynwood Walls in Miami, Florida

A few days after the kids' depositions, I heard back from the district attorney. Kenny was taking a plea deal. There would be no trial. He was pleading guilty to third-degree felony battery by strangulation.

They scheduled our court date for the end of January for us to give our victim's impact statement and for sentencing.

We made the trek back across Alligator Alley for the trial. The kids and I didn't say much on the ride over.

"Do either of you need to write your statements down?" I asked them.

Madisson said she had something written out on her phone. Brendon said he didn't need to write it down. I had written a four-page statement to read at the hearing. None of us discussed what would be said. We were just grateful it was coming to an end. We planned to go to a local Escape Room afterward to decompress.

Walking into the courthouse, I saw our local news reporter from the NBC station with her cameraperson in tow. She was there to cover the hearing. Madisson asked her not to put her on camera. When we walked into the courtroom, Kenny wasn't present. They escorted him in just before the hearing started. I was on edge. My hands were shaking.

When we all approached the podium to face the judge, Kenny's attorney stated he was agreeing to a plea deal.

When the judge said he didn't want to see the video of the assault, I quickly spoke up to ask that he reconsider prior to passing down his sentence. He agreed.

With my kids and me on one side and Ken and his attorney on the other, it was awkward. I couldn't bring myself to look his way. After the video played, we were allowed to give our victim impact statements.

I read mine with a shaky voice through my tears.

Madisson took the opportunity to show just how angry she was.

"I hate you!" she said. "I hope you rot in hell."

Her remarks were unfiltered, and I was proud of her for having the courage to say exactly how she felt.

Brendon finished his remarks by saying, "What I heard that night was a monster. What he did is unforgivable."

Unfortunately, district attorney offices do not typically take cases to trial if they don't think they can win, so many cases are never tried. Florida works on a point system to determine jail time.

Before the judge handed down sentencing, he thanked my ex-husband for his service as a public safety officer. The judge gave him points for his years of service in the fire department.

He missed having to go to jail by one point.

How convenient.

I hadn't realized that the attorneys had taken felony battery off the table. He was not being tried in civil court. Instead, it was family court so the sentencing would be lighter.

I will never understand why this assault was tried in family court. Assault is assault. The fact that we had been married prior should not have made the sentence lighter, but it did.

He received one year of house arrest and three years of probation. He had to wear a GPS ankle monitoring bracelet. A no-contact order went into effect until after he had served his probation.

When I asked about a permanent restraining order, I was told I would have to pursue that in the county I lived in. The entire experience was frustrating. Having gone through it, I understand now why so many women decide not to press charges. I felt like I was pushing a boulder up a mountain.

I wanted to make sure my children and I would never have to worry about him again. I filed for a permanent restraining order in Lee County, Florida. The attorney given to me by Abuse Counseling and Treatment said it was virtually impossible to get a permanent one. I told him to please try.

The day prior to our trial, Kenny offered me a permanent restraining order but refused to give one to my children.

I refused.

He then countered with a permanent order for me and five years for the kids.

I refused again.

It was clear he wanted to make getting a permanent order difficult for us. I called every reporter I knew and asked them to attend my hearing. They at least owed me that considering I had been their news story for the past five years.

I had no idea whether they would cover the story, but I knew having them at court would put pressure on Kenny. My son didn't attend the hearing. He was tired of going to court. Madisson had to drive down from Tampa, where she was attending college at the University of South Florida. Attending these hearings was a huge time commitment.

The news media showed up, and their presence worked. As soon as Kenny entered the courtroom and saw the media, his attorney asked to approach the judge. My attorney returned with great news.

"Ken has agreed to a permanent restraining order for all three of you," he said.

I was grateful and relieved.

"You need to carry the injunction with you in your car or purse, because once you cross into another county or state, there's no way for the police to pull up the order," I was told.

In addition to physical and psychological abuse from Kenny, I suffered economic abuse as well. He had used my credit cards to pay for our hotels and restaurant bills throughout the year we were together. He paid off the card, then ran it up again.

Prior to the assault, we had been planning to move to Pompano Beach together when my term ended. I had put down a security deposit on a condominium a week prior as Kenny did not have a checking account. I eventually got my money back; however, I had to show documentation as to why, which was humiliating.

It was difficult for me to find work after leaving office due to the media coverage of my assault, and I had to use the rest of my credit line to live. It did not take long for my second card to reach the limit. As if going through the ordeal had not been enough, in December 2019 I was forced to file for bankruptcy.

The entire experience left me angry, but also worried. I worried about other women unknowingly dating him and being put through the same ordeal as my family. Feeling robbed of justice, I made a pact with myself. I would do whatever I had to do to make sure his actions showed up on every internet search of him. He had had his court records sealed so no one could read the case. That didn't stop me from putting as much information as I could about him online.

In March 2018, I was asked to come to New York to appear on HLN's television show *Crime & Justice with Ashleigh Banfield*. I was live in the studio for a ten-minute segment on my case and his sentencing. I wanted to reach as many women as I could to share my story in hopes that others in similar situations would find the courage to leave.

I was nervous about sharing my story; however, the messages I received from women all over the US showed me the topic was an important one. I was determined to change the narrative around the type of woman who finds herself in an abusive relationship.

Mayor Sawicki on *Crime & Justice with Ashleigh Banfield*.

One in three women will be victims of domestic violence. On average, over 1,500 women die at the hand of their abuser each year. It's a public health crisis no one talks about. If I could help shine even a dim light on a problem no one wants to discuss, putting myself out there to tell my story was worth it.

In 2020, my efforts paid off. A woman that Kenny started dating just two months after the assault contacted me on LinkedIn. It took me a few weeks to get the nerve up to email her back. Once we were on the phone, she was distraught. She wanted to ask me questions about our relationship. Reluctantly I agreed to speak with her.

She was an executive at her company and owned her own home. Ken had done the same things to her as he did to me. Her mother had just passed away and she was now losing her home due to being in so much debt. I did my best to reassure her that life continues and that she would get through this. When we hung up, I said a prayer hoping she would not return to him.

I never heard from her again.

The FDLE and Ethics Commission issued their findings in March as well. Not guilty. The final report stated clearly that I had not violated any Florida statutes. They said there was no probable cause that I had wrongly accepted gifts from Brian Rist, no probable cause that I had accepted gifts of value that influenced my vote, and no probable cause that I had failed to file a statement disclosing gifts over one hundred dollars. "Accordingly, this complaint is dismissed with the issuance of this public report," it said.

There was no evidence of any wrongdoing. The state attorney advised the FDLE that the case would be dropped for "insufficient evidence to prove criminal law violation" with no further action.

This was the day I had been waiting for. I could finally put it all behind me.

Unfortunately, the news media had lost interest. They ran a few articles saying I had been found not guilty. It turns out it's more sensational to report that the mayor's office is under investigation than to share the findings that I hadn't done anything wrong.

It was frustrating.

One article ran on March 18, 2018, by the local NBC station was titled "Investigation Reveals Former Firefighter Wanted Cape Mayor Out of Office."

"The Cape Coral Fire Department opened an internal investigation in May 2017 regarding former lieutenant firefighter Kenneth Retzer for making derogatory, demeaning and insulting comments about city council members, former mayor Marni Sawicki and city employees," the article stated.

The story that aired was less than a minute. Articles in the newspaper ran only once.

Meanwhile, Ken had no issues moving on. I found out that he used his retirement money to buy a new fishing boat and start the next chapter of his life. He moved to Pompano Beach, Florida, and now offers chartered fishing trips. He owns Epic Blue Adventures. Even with his felony charges, the Coast Guard issued him a Master Six-Pack license so he can take people out one hundred miles off the coast. To this day I have no idea whether his guns were returned to him. With the felony battery charge dropped, I suspect they have been.

The people I had considered friends throughout my term as mayor disappeared after I left office. I had helped a woman named Jennifer Nelson get elected to replace council member Richard Leon. After the assault, she had asked me to move in with her while I went through the trial process. I helped her craft her message for her campaign and introduced her to all my important donors.

After she won her election, I asked her if she could get me two VIP tickets to the city's Red, White, & Boom Fourth of July event, the same event that Brian Rist sponsored. She emailed me to tell me she could not get the tickets and needed to use all of hers for her daughter and her friends.

That was the last time I spoke to her. I heard later that she changed her party affiliation from Democrat to Republican.

Janis, my campaign manager, and Lynn, who owned Dixie Roadhouse, also stopped returning my calls.

Brian Rist went back to his wife for the ninth time. He did not like the idea of giving her half of everything he had worked for. They are still together today.

Mayor Kevin Ruane ran for county commissioner of Lee County and won. He now lives in Cape Coral and continues to fight for water quality. We have spoken a few times since I left office.

In 2021, while still seated, council member John Carioscia succumbed to COVID-19.

Councilmember Jim Burch and I still speak periodically. He doesn't regret his decision not to run for reelection.

Mayor Joe Coviello passed away a year after taking office from a heart attack.

Michel Doherty, my mentor and dear friend, passed away in 2021 at the age of ninety-six. I still miss her. I like to believe she is watching over me.

My other mentor throughout my campaign, Alex LePera, took Kenny's side prior to his court date. She didn't believe he was capable of physical violence. Even after the video was released showing his erratic and violent behavior, she never again spoke to me.

Council member Jessica Cosden was elected for a second term, and governing board member Sam Fisher ran for a seat on the Lee County School Board in 2022. He also switched his party to Republican after being a longtime Democrat. Ironically, Governor Ron DeSantis endorsed him as a "pro-parent candidate" even though he has no children of his own. Neither suffered any consequences for their part in Kenny and Kirsten's attempt to take me down.

Kirsten Thompson disappeared into the background. Graham Morris lost his bid for city council in 2013 and again in 2017. Former council members Rana Erbrick and Richard Leon also stepped out of the limelight. After losing her bid for mayor, Rana moved to Fort Myers. Richard moved to Bonita Springs after he lost his reelection bid.

On September 28, 2022, Hurricane Ian tore a path of destruction through Cape Coral. Recovery of the area will take years.

Looking back over those past years, so much has changed for me. When I was in the middle of the chaos, it was difficult to see the path forward. It was also difficult to look inward.

I love Dr. Dyer's quote: "If you change the way you look at things, the things you look at change."

While I would never choose to go through what I did again, I know I am a better person for going through it. Over time I have realized there are no victims in life—only volunteers.

I certainly don't mean to minimize anyone who is currently in a situation of abuse. But I have realized that the only person who could have allowed the abuse to happen to me was me. My lack of self-worth and self-love allowed someone like Kenny to come into my life.

If you've ever taken a motorcycle class, the instructor tells you not to concentrate on any object on the side of the road, because looking at it will cause you to hit it. This is the best analogy I can think of when describing how I ended up staying in such an unhealthy relationship for so long. I spent years in therapy trying to understand why things happened the way they did in my childhood and afterward.

I had let the abuse and lack of self-worth become part of who I was. And while I thought it gave me strength, mostly what it did was give me an excuse to focus on factors outside of my control. I looked everywhere else instead of focusing on what I could control. By focusing on the bad things, I ended up veering off into harmful behaviors and relationships over and over and over, like hitting the object on the side of the road.

Learning to focus on today and to love my life as it is today has changed me beyond words. Clearing those negative things out of my life has allowed me to focus on what I really want—joy and happiness.

Realizing that my today is only an accumulation of past events has allowed me to forgive myself and others. I am creating my future one day at a time. The starting point is not yesterday; it is today. Understanding this over time has led to every day being better than the one before. As I've practiced this way of thinking, clarity has given me the courage to stay away from those who do not offer me joy and happiness.

I used to think people don't change. Now I see that we change every day. The clock resets every morning, giving us the opportunity to choose a different path.

Having been asked many times what I want my legacy to be, here is what I know so far: I know I have made mistakes, and I am okay with them. I have grown more through those mistakes than I ever would have by behaving as others thought I should or by being what they thought I should be. I can hold my head up high, understanding that my strength and resolve have made an impact—and I don't need to worry about how much of an impact.

I have raised two amazingly strong, loving children who know their worth and understand that if they don't like something, they have the power to change it. If my children are my only contribution in this lifetime, I've done my part.

I know the smallest gesture of kindness can change a person's life. It has changed mine many times.

I know I don't have all the answers. Sometimes it's the ride that matters.

I know I've had my heart broken by lovers as well as friends; however, I now understand that people come into your life to teach you specific life lessons, and not all of them are meant to stay forever. Without them, my growth would never have been possible.

I know that what others think of me does not define me. In fact, the louder people call out my shortcomings, the more impact I know I've made. Refusing to make myself small so others can feel big is my true purpose.

I know I can't control other people's bad behavior, only how I react. Choosing to believe they are doing the best they can has allowed me to forgive and let go.

I know we are stronger together. Lifting others up is a true sign of my comfort in my own skin and the love I have for myself.

And finally, I know that well-behaved women seldom make history.

About the Authors

The Honorable Marni Sawicki

Marni Sawicki is the former mayor of Cape Coral, Florida. The city is currently the sixth-largest city in the state and home to over 190,000 people. She was elected in 2013 and served for four years.

Marni holds an MBA and has held numerous positions in business such as general manager, operations manager, and vice president of marketing. She founded her own consulting business in 2013, Indigo Pros.

In 2015, she was awarded the Elected Women of Excellence Award by the National Foundation of Women Legislators (NFWL) and received two Home Rule Hero Awards from the Florida League of Cities for her work advocating on behalf of her city. She also received the Ally for Equality Award from Equality Florida (Human Rights Campaign) in 2014 for being the first mayor in southwest Florida to sign the Freedom to Marry resolution. Mayor Sawicki championed the effort to streamline the city's Strategic Plan while working alongside the city manager to develop a balanced scorecard, adding a new level of accountability to local government.

Throughout her career, Marni has made a point to give back through volunteering for various women's veterans organizations. As a survivor of domestic violence, one of her missions is to inspire others in situations of abuse to stand up and safely get out.

Peter Golenbock

Peter Golenbock, one of the nation's best-known sports authors, graduated from Dartmouth College in 1967 and the NYU School of Law in 1970. He has written seven *New York Times* bestsellers, including *The Bronx Zoo* (with Sparky Lyle) and *American Prince* (with Tony Curtis).